'Offering advice on choos ......
encourage and when to pu ......
of sex with slaves, and whe ......
Manage your Slaves provides ....man's-eye view of an
ancient world very different to our own.' *Daily Telegraph*

'Packed with fascinating references to the earliest
writings about slavery' *Independent*

'In his Machiavellian guide, Falx (with the ironical
help of Cambridge classicist Jerry Toner) ponders the
politics, philosophy and social conventions of being a
noble Roman.' *Saga*

'Captivating' *Bloomberg News*

MARCUS SIDONIUS FALX is a Roman of noble birth, whose
family have kept slaves for generations. After serving
with distinction in the legions, he retired to manage his
substantial country estates. Marcus now divides his time
between his land in Campania and the province of Africa
and his luxury villa on the Esquiline hill overlooking
Rome. He holds many strong and rather unpalatable
views which he refuses to acknowledge may be wrong.
In order to make his book more accessible for a non-
Roman audience, he has employed the services of DR
JERRY TONER, Fellow and Director of Classics at Churchill
College, Cambridge University, to set his work in context
and provide guidance for readers who want to know
more about its fascinating if disagreeable subject.

HOW TO MANAGE YOUR SLAVES

MARCUS SIDONIUS FALX

Commentary by Jerry Toner
Foreword by Mary Beard

P

PROFILE BOOKS

This paperback edition published in 2015

First published in Great Britain in 2014 by
PROFILE BOOKS LTD
3 Holford Yard
Bevin Way
London WC1X 9HD
www.profilebooks.com

3 5 7 9 10 8 6 4

Typeset in Bembo by MacGuru Ltd
info@macguru.org.uk

Printed and bound in Great Britain by
CPI Group (UK) Ltd, Croydon CR0 4YY

A CIP catalogue record for this book is available from the British Library.

ISBN 978 1 78125 252 9
eISBN 978 1 78283 054 2

CONTENTS

FOREWORD

I HAVE NEVER COME ACROSS Marcus Sidonius Falx before, but I know his type. The Roman world had plenty of people just like him who owned huge numbers of slaves and who, for most of the time, did not give slavery a second thought. It was completely normal, a natural part of the social order. But the Romans did think about slaves in their own way: how they could control them, and how best to show them off to their friends. And the smarter ones (and that might include Falx here) could actually be a bit scared. They worried about what the slaves were up to behind their backs, and where the battle lines of ancient Roman culture were drawn. 'All slaves are enemies' ran one famous Roman slogan, well known to Falx. And on a notorious occasion in the reign of the emperor Nero, a Roman plutocrat was murdered by one of his 400 household slaves. It didn't, as you will see, make Falx rest entirely easy in his bed, but the whole household was put to death as punishment.

I am a bit surprised that Falx and Toner got on so well. Falx is an aristocrat whereas Toner's family – so he assures me – has its roots in those classes oppressed by the British elite ('from an Irish potato field' I'm told).

But it is to the credit of both of them, I guess, that they seem to have hit it off, despite their political differences. Of course, there were slave owners of a very different sort from Falx. There were thousands of small traders and craftsmen who owned just one or two slaves. And very many of them were freed – and actually married those who had once been their owners, both male and female. Even in Falx's league, there were a few favored slave secretaries and PA's who lived better than poor free Romans trying to make a living on day labour at the docks, or selling cheap flowers in the Forum. Interestingly some of the free poor got onto the streets to demonstrate, unsuccessfully, against the (strictly legal) punishment of those 400 slaves. But Falx is talking about the use of mass slave labour.

It is hard for us now to understand all the dimensions of the relations between free, and slave, and ex-slave (and it was hard then). But we do have a few glimpses of what the rich Romans thought of their ordinary slave-workers; and Falx is one of the most reliable guides we have to what Romans would have seen as a proud tradition of 'slave management'. He is trying to help everyone share the benefits of his wisdom, and he is a good place to learn.

Thankfully the world has moved on. But his text offers an authentic insight – as authentic as you can get – into a fundamental aspect of life in Rome and its empire. If it had been published 2,000 years ago it would have topped the management charts. Modern readers may have trouble mastering their prejudices; but underneath the buoyant rhetoric, they'll maybe find Falx not a wholly bad man, by the standards of his day at least.

And Falx points the finger at us too. Do some of his insights still help us manage our own 'staff'. For are we sure that 'wage-slaves' are really so much different from 'slaves'? How different are we from the Romans?

Mary Beard
Cambridge, April 2014

AUTHOR'S NOTE

MY NAME IS MARCUS SIDONIUS FALX, of noble birth, whose great-great-grandfather held a consul-ship, and whose mother hails from an ancient senator-ial lineage. Our family was given the name Falx – 'the Claw' – for our stubborn refusal to let anything go. I served with distinction in the Legio VI 'Ironclad' for five years, campaigning mostly against troublesome oriental tribes, before returning to Rome to run my affairs and my substantial estates in Campania and the province of Africa. My family has owned countless slaves for count-less generations. There is nothing we do not know about the management of them.

In order to write for a non-Roman audience I have been compelled to use the services of a certain Jerry Toner, a teacher in one of our miserable northern prov-inces, who knows something of our Roman ways but shares few of our virtues. Indeed a man so soft I have never encountered outside the servile class: he has not once fought in battle, can scarce drink a small amphora of watered wine, and even stoops so low that he himself will clean his baby's backside rather than leave such foul tasks to the slaves and womenfolk. He is, however, most

blessed to be married to a wife of great beauty and intellect (though she is perhaps more forward with her opinions than a woman ought to be), to whom I am most
grateful for ensuring that the meaning of my text is clear
for you barbarian readers.

Marcus Sidonius Falx
Rome, pridie Idus Martias

COMMENTATOR'S NOTE

MARCUS SIDONIUS FALX'S existence may be the subject of academic debate, but the reality of his opinions is beyond doubt. They provide a Roman's-eye view of slavery. Slavery was a core institution of the Roman world for the whole of its existence. It was so central that it never occurred to anyone that it might not exist. Owning slaves was as normal as voting Conservative in Wiltshire or Labour in Hampstead. Sadly, we don't know what the slaves themselves thought, because their views didn't matter. But we know plenty about what their Roman masters thought of them. The substance of Marcus's words survives in Roman texts on slavery, although he has not followed them slavishly. These sources are often obscure or quite hard to interpret. This single text is his clear and simple manual for managing slaves the Roman way. Needless to say the fact that I have helped bring it to publication does not mean that I approve of it.

Marcus has been a difficult author to work with. He holds many strong and unpalatable views that he refuses to acknowledge may be wrong or immoral. But by Roman standards, Marcus was a decent man. His text shows how the Roman world, for all its apparent familiarity, can be almost casually shocking. It also shows how complex an institution was slavery.

Marcus has refused to reveal his age: his opinions are often an amalgam of views from across the centuries, although he appears to have taken them mostly from the empire of the first and second centuries AD. I have added brief commentaries to his words at the end of each chapter to give some context to his advice and (at least partly for the sake of my own reputation) to contradict some of his more unreconstructed views. These, with the further reading at the end of the book, will point those who are interested in digging deeper towards the underlying primary sources and modern discussions.

Jerry Toner
Cambridge, April 2014

· INTRODUCTION ·

BE THE MASTER

A REMARKABLE THING happened to me in the gardens of my villa some months ago. It was an event so strange and thought-provoking that it caused me to write this book. I happened to be entertaining a guest from one of the German tribes, an Alan to be precise. You may well wonder what a man of my rank was doing playing host to a miserable barbarian, but this man was no normal German. He was a prince who had come to our great city of Rome as part of an embassy to the emperor. Tired of having to find small talk concerning the benefits of trousers, and other such tedious issues which interest their sort, our great leader had asked me to house his foreign visitor until his return to that foul swamp he calls home.

We were taking a casual walk in the extensive parterre at the back of my villa and I was explaining to my guest, in simple Latin so as not to confuse him, what various mythological heroes the many marble statues represented. Then this happened. Concentrating my attention on the statuary, I failed to notice a small hoe lying in the pathway. As I stood on the metal end, the wooden handle sprang up into my shins, causing me to cry out, more in alarm than pain. A certain slave, who was standing nearby and whose tool it was, smirked as he saw me hop about on one leg. Naturally I was outraged that this worthless idiot, a man who is himself nothing more than a tool that can speak, should laugh at his master's mishap. I summoned the bailiff.

'This slave thinks that injuries to the leg are amusing. Let us break his legs and see how much he laughs.'

That wiped the smile from his face. Ignoring the pitiful begging which slaves always resort to when faced with their just deserts, the bailiff and two sturdy attendants pulled the man down to the ground, while a fourth ran over with a heavy iron bar. Just as he was raising the implement above his head, my barbarian guest cried out, 'No!'

Turning to confront him, I saw that he was as white as a freshly sulphured toga.

'What is the matter?'

He hesitated. I pressed him:

'Surely you would treat your slaves the same way?'

'We do not have slaves,' was his extraordinary reply.

Imagine that? A society without slaves! Who has ever heard of such a thing! How would it function? Who would perform the basest tasks, those that are beneath even the lowest-born free man? What would you do with all those captives acquired in wars of conquest? How would you display your wealth? With my mind turning over all these imponderable questions, I found my anger softening.

'Please, master, I beg you …' whimpered the slave.

'Oh all right …'

I told the bailiff to stop and let the slave off with a light beating with rods. I know, I know, I am too soft. But so many owners today are far too quick to punish their slaves brutally for very minor offences. It is always better to count to ten before you act.

Leading my troubled guest back towards the house, it occurred to me that this German barbarian might not be alone in being unused to owning slaves. With so many in the world now addicted to vulgar equality, it became clear to me that people no longer understand how to treat their slaves and underlings properly. I decided, therefore, to set down the principles with which any free person can ensure the efficient running of their attendants.

This is a vitally important task. The man who devotes himself to personal advancement through the acquisition of power and wealth should understand everything that will help him in this endeavour. It never ceases to amaze me how many in authority today have no inkling of how best to treat those who are so fortunate as to serve them in their ambition. Instead, desperately seeking to ingratiate themselves with those whose loyalty should be in no doubt, they fawn and pander to even the lowest sort of humanity. I have even seen a leading politician smile warmly at a woman working in the street in a pathetic attempt to win her worthless support. Knowledge of how to treat the basest in society, which can be acquired from the careful study of this work, will, by contrast, provide the wherewithal to achieve glory. It will teach the means to attain the goal of a household that is fully in accord with its master's wishes. This will provide a secure power base from which to rise in society. The book will impart the social skills with which to command those who will come to report to you as your reputation burgeons. Accordingly, any attentive head of a household, whose heart is set on pursuing a leadership role, is strongly advised to take special pains to consult my work, which is the fruit of one of the most experienced heads of the ancient past.

I believe that there is a science of how to be a master, which proves that running a household and controlling slaves is the same as being a leader in wider society. Whether leaders and masters are not also born is impossible to answer with any certainty. Some Greeks have argued that all men differ from each other according to their inner natures. Those who do manual, physical work are slavish by nature, and it is better for them to come under the control of people such as myself who are in possession of natures of a higher sort. For a man who is capable of belonging to another person is, by nature, a slave; and that is why, the argument goes, such a man belongs to someone else. Nature, they say, clearly also intended to make the bodies and souls of free men different to those of slaves. Slaves have bodies that are strong and well suited to the kind of physical services they have to do. Their souls are less capable of reasoning. The bodies of free men, by contrast, are upright and not much use for that kind of manual work. But their souls are intelligent. They are suited for the purposes of partaking in the life of the community, whether it be political or military. Of course, nature sometimes makes mistakes and the opposite happens – slaves are given the bodies of free men, free men only the souls and not the bodies of free men. But on the whole, the Greeks said, nature does not make mistakes. She makes sure that each is allotted a nature suitable to his fate in life.

But most Romans disagree with this. They believe that controlling another human being is contrary to nature. So many of us Romans who continue to rule a great empire are now descended from slaves that it would be ridiculous to believe that slaves are inherently useless. Roman thinkers argue that it is only social convention that leads one man to own another as a slave. They say that there is no natural difference between the two. It is a simple injustice, one that is based on the use of force. They also rightly point out that many slaves have acted in a brave and noble way during times of great crisis, which shows that they are not all slavish by nature. And if slavery is not natural then neither is being a master. It must be learnt!

Rome is full of slaves. I have heard it said that as many as one in three or four of the inhabitants of the Italian peninsula are in servitude. Even in the vast expanse of the empire as a whole, whose population cannot fall far short of 60 or 70 million persons, perhaps as many as one in eight is a slave. Nor are these slaves only to be found in the rural areas. Rome is teeming with every kind of slave activity and its servile population is as high as anywhere. Perhaps a million live in the capital city, and some claim that at least a third of them are slaves. While such estimates represent little more than the informed guesswork of those with overactive imaginations, it tells you how important an institution slavery is for the Roman world. We Romans need our slaves.

You may well ask how this situation came about. What were the advantages in using slaves instead of free labour? Let me explain. In the past, during the republic, whenever the Romans had conquered a region of Italy, they took part of the land for themselves and populated it with Roman settlers. They intended these colonies to act as garrison towns. But much land was left empty and unfarmed as a result of the fighting. This was either because the owners had been killed or had fled while fighting in the army against us Romans. The senate proclaimed that anyone who wanted to farm this land could do so in return for a payment of 10 per cent of the annual harvest of cereal crops and 20 per cent of the fruit crops. The aim was to increase the population of Italy, who would, by dint of their hard work, produce more food for cities and also act as soldiers to fight for Rome in times of war.

Such fine intentions! But the result was the very opposite of what they sought to achieve. What happened was that the rich got hold of most of that land which was not distributed as allotments, and, once they had grown used to owning this land and felt comfortable that no one would snatch it back from them, they persuaded the poor peasants who owned smallholdings next to their own to sell them. Or, if the peasants refused, they sometimes simply seized the land violently. There was nothing that a poor farmer could do to defend himself against such a powerful neighbour, often because he was himself away on active service. Bit by bit, the large holdings grew until they became vast estates instead of simple farms. The estate owners did not want to rely on the very farmers they had dispossessed to farm their land, nor did they wish to employ free men to labour for them since they would almost certainly be called away at some point to serve in the army. So they bought slaves and relied on them. This proved to be a very profitable exercise, in particular because the slaves bred and produced many children. And the beauty of it was that none of these slaves was liable for military service, since the army naturally cannot rely on slaves to serve in defence of the state. The estate owners became extremely wealthy. At the same time, the number of slaves grew rapidly. But the number of Italians became fewer and those few that there were grew poorer, oppressed as they were by taxes and by the burden of long military service. Even during those brief periods of leave when they were not on military service, the freeborn could find no work because the land was owned by the rich and they used slaves to work it instead of free labour.

Naturally, the senate and the Roman people grew anxious that they would no longer be able to call upon enough Italian troops and that this great body of slaves would destroy their masters. But they could also see that it would be neither easy nor equitable to take these huge estates away from their owners, since they had been in their possession now for generations. How do you dispossess a man of a tree that his grandfather planted with his own hand? Some of the tribunes of the people brought in laws to try to limit the size of such estates and force the great landowners to employ a certain proportion of free men. But no one took any notice of these laws. As to the threat of slaves, the worry was not so much that they would revolt, but that they would eradicate the freeborn peasant, on whom the Roman elite relied to serve in the army and keep them in power. So it was decreed that no citizen over twenty years of age and under forty should serve in the army outside of Italy for more than three years at a time in order to give them a chance to keep control of their smallholdings at home.

Thankfully, the slave owner today need not trouble himself with such concerns. The army is now professional and it is many, many years since there has been a great slave revolt. Today's slave owner needs to worry only about keeping control of his own household. These are matters that I picked up at my father's knee. As a lad, I learnt to command authority, issuing my string of attendants with their orders: 'Bring me my cloak!', 'Wash my hands!', 'Serve me my breakfast, boy!' were the commands that punctuated my daily life. And as a callow youth, my father taught me how to instil respect into even the most recalcitrant slave.

The household is the cornerstone of society and, indeed, all human life. No kind of civilised existence is possible at all without the acquisition of the basic necessities that the household provides. But a household is just a house if it has no slaves. To be sure, a family needs a wife and children. Indeed, we can profit from their work. But it is the slaves who provide the bulk of the services. This is particularly beneficial because it means the master of the household does not have to rely on outsiders to provide those services. We all know how degrading it is to have to ask others for help and how tiresome to bring in external contractors to do jobs for us. They never turn up when instructed to, take liberties with their fees, and, taking little pride in their work, carry out their tasks shoddily. With slaves, however, we can be sure that work will be carried out in just the way that we want it to be done. The slaves, therefore, turn the family unit into a much more significant unit, that is to say, the household.

The household is like a miniature version of the state itself, with its own structure, hierarchy and leadership and its own sense of community. Husband/wife, father/son, master/slave are the basic building blocks of social life. As such, slavery is one of the key principles of social organisation. The slave is at the complete disposal of the master of the household, in the same way that the citizen must obey the commands of the state. But slavery is a state of absolute subjection. The slave has no kin, he cannot assume the rights and obligations of marriage, his very identity is imposed by the owner, who gives him his name. Slavery is the same as social death in this respect. Complete submission is expected. Regrettably, slaves sometimes have to be coerced and worn down into obedience. Their spirit has to be broken. It is for this reason that some of the prouder tribes refuse ever to surrender when defeated in battle. The Cantabri in Spain, for example, killed themselves after the failure of their revolt rather than suffer enslavement.

All slaves share the same lack of legal rights. But we should not assume that they only perform tasks that are beneath the free man. In fact, as we shall also see, many slaves have acquired positions of influence on account of the power of their masters. Equally, many poor free men have to carry out the most loathsome tasks in order to put bread before their families. Slaves are also used to carry out a bewildering array of tasks. Whether it is the old retainer keeping watch on the front door, or the young boy serving water at table, or the comely slave girl attending in the bed-chamber, slaves carry out a wide variety of jobs within a large household that minister to the master's every need.

My father taught me what slaves were also for — showing off! Slaves may be morally worthless, mere things and possessions, but despite this they confer high status upon their owners. In the same way that a fine horse reflects well upon its rider, so a well-mannered and deferential slave highlights the merits of its owner. And if there are four hundred of them in the household, then how much greater is the glory which is displayed! Who but the highest in society can afford to maintain so impressive and prestigious a retinue?

For slaves might be dullards but they serve the noblest. If you want to learn how you too should treat those slaves who accrue to you as your good fortune grows, then read on. For however much the practice of your own times is at variance with the principles of the ancient world, that should not discourage you from learning from them. For in the works of the ancients far more is to be found to merit your approval than your rejection. Read and learn.

·· COMMENTARY ··

The story that the Alan tribe did not have slaves shows how remarkable such a fact was to a Roman writer. The fourth-century AD historian Ammianus felt it was worth recording precisely because it would have struck his Roman audience as curious at best. There are no examples of Romans arguing that slavery should be abolished. It was a simple fact of social life, in the same way that owning a car or a cat is today. Wealthy Romans saw slaves as being necessary for a high standard of living, just as we view modern domestic appliances. Slaves did all the things that you would not want to do yourself – washing, cleaning, even wiping your backside – as well as providing a whole range of other services. But not all slaves were alike. There was a big difference between domestic slaves in the city and the slaves working in the fields. Urban slaves were as much about status as efficiency, in much the same way as are many modern household possessions (do we really need that 100-inch plasma TV?). Even country slaves may not always have been kept primarily for economic reasons, even though their roles were crucial, especially in the large estates of the rich.

The Greeks held a stronger view of the nature of slaves than did the Romans. Aristotle famously argued that slaves were naturally slavish, and it was right for them to be owned by the superior Greeks. Athenian society maintained a strong divide between citizen and slave, which made it difficult for slaves to be assimilated into society even when they were freed. A completely different model operated in Rome, where large numbers of outsiders were habitually assimilated into its ranks of citizens. One of the main reasons for Rome's great success was its ability to incorporate all manner of foreigners and their gods. This allowed it to expand its pool of man-power along with its territory. In such a society, it made no sense to exclude slaves permanently from becoming Roman. Instead it seemed more sensible to think of slavery as a temporary state, after which, if the right attitude had been shown, a slave could achieve Roman citizenship. Somewhat surprisingly, Roman slavery was as much about social mobility as structural rigidity.

Slaves had few legal rights in Roman law but this was not adhered to rigorously, especially in urban households. It was usual for city slaves to be allowed to own money and possessions, even if this *peculium* legally remained the property of the owner. Although slaves could not marry, in practice they were often allowed to form partnerships. They acquired more legal rights during the empire: for example they could appeal to the emperor's statue for sanctuary from an abusive master. But this increased level of imperial interest did not mean that the emperors wanted to improve slaves' conditions. As supreme leaders, they simply came to interfere in all kinds of issues. People looked to them to provide guidance and rulings about what was legally acceptable in all manner of domestic matters.

Numbers regarding the quantity of slaves in the Roman world need to be treated with caution. They are informed guesses at best. The surviving evidence is poor and also pretty thin. You can find discussion of the numbers and degree of social mobility of slaves in Roman Italy in Walter Scheidel's 'Human Mobility in Roman Italy, II: The Slave Population', in the *Journal of Roman Studies*, 95 (2005), 64–79, and 'The slave population of Roman Italy: speculation and constraints', in *Topoi*, 9 (1999), 129–44.

For the story that the Alans were notable for not having any slaves, see Ammianus Marcellinus 31.2.25. Seneca complains that owners who get angry are too quick to punish their slaves with whippings and by having their legs broken for very minor offences such as answering back or giving them cheeky looks: see *On Anger* 3.24 and 32. The explanation for Marcus's aims of this book is based on the preface of Columella's work, *On Agriculture*. The legal status of slaves can be found in the *Digest* 1.5. Aristotle *Politics* 1.2 contains the discussion about the household, slaves as tools, and whether slaves are so by nature. For the ancient analysis of why slave numbers increased in Italy, see Appian, *Civil Wars*, 1.1; this can be usefully compared with the modern analysis of Keith Hopkins in the first chapter of his *Conquerors and Slaves*.

CHAPTER I

HOW TO BUY A SLAVE

I F A SCULPTOR WISHES to make a great work of art he begins by searching out the piece of stone that most perfectly suits his purpose. So too the slave owner must realise that it is only from the right kind of human material that he can ever hope to fashion slaves who display the desirable characteristics of cheerfulness, hard work and obedience. It is vital that he takes the greatest care in selecting the best slaves in the market, ensuring that they are free from defects, whether physical, mental or moral. Here I shall instruct you how best to go about the difficult task of buying a slave.

Firstly, the where. Many will tell you to go to the Roman forum, behind the temple of Castor, but you would do well to ignore their advice. Only the lowest and roughest sorts of slave are offered for sale there. Far better are those to be found from the slave traders who operate in the Saepta Julia, close by the Pantheon. This is particularly so if you are seeking to buy a soft boy, or something from one of the more exotic regions of the empire or even beyond, from such places as Ethiopia. All of these are to be found among the traders there, although you must be sure to ask them directly if they have anything special tucked away in the back of their shops. They always keep their best hidden from public view so as to retain them for their premium customers. You will have no trouble finding a castrated boy there too, if that is your desire, even though the law in theory prohibits such a trade.

Legally speaking, slaves are either captives from war or descended from female slaves but in reality there are other avenues into servitude. Some of the destitute illegally sell themselves into slavery to clear debts, or they might sell one of their children to help feed the remaining offspring. It is common practice for people to abandon unwanted babies at the rubbish dump on the edge of town and people sometimes raise these abandoned infants as their own slaves, even though such children technically remain freeborn. It is also to be suspected that slave dealers often buy their wares from traders who have simply kidnapped their goods, using pirate raids to snatch adults and children from far-flung coastal regions.

There is no doubt at all, however, concerning the legitimacy of those whom our armies have captured in war. These individuals owe their very lives to the mercy of our soldiers who chose, in the flush of victory, not to massacre them but spare their miserable lives so that they might provide us with services as payback for their military resistance. Captives from the wealthiest families might be given back to them after the payment of a satisfactory ransom. The rest pay for their lives through slavery.

I myself once took part in the sack of a small city in the border region with the Persian empire. After initial attempts to persuade the inhabitants to surrender peacefully in return for their lives had failed, we attacked vigorously and quickly broke through the city wall with our battering rams. Gaining control of the suburbs, we began to slaughter anyone we came across, whether man, woman or child. Most of the inhabitants fled into the old part of the city, in the centre, from where they sent out ambassadors in order to try to save their lives. What fools they had been not to accept our generous offer before. It was agreed that those who could pay the equivalent of 2,000 sesterces could go free, and fourteen thousand were in a position to do that. The rest, who amounted to some thirteen thousand, as well as all the other booty we could obtain, were sold.

Our commander was generous enough to distribute half of the slaves to us as a reward for our loyal service during the campaign. The rest he sold for the benefit of the state, to pay for the erection of a small votive shrine in gratitude to the gods for our victory, and for his own financial gain. The numbers involved here were, of course, nothing in comparison to the great booties which the likes of Julius Caesar acquired from his conquests. He is reputed to have taken one million slaves captive in Gaul. Or the mass enslavements which took place after the capture of Jerusalem, when it seemed that nearly the entire Jewish race fell into servitude, or in Dacia, when the great Trajan subjugated that warlike people. No, ours was small beer by comparison.

Once a slave has become a slave, by no matter which

route, if he is to be sold he will in time find himself in one of the aforementioned slave-dealer shops. There the slaves will generally be stood on a raised platform to ensure that prospective buyers are able to have a good look at them. Those who are newly imported have their feet chalked white. Other information, regarding his or her place of birth and personal characteristics, will be found on a label hung round the slave's neck.

The sale of slaves is regulated by the relevant sections of the Curule Aediles' Edict. The purpose of this is to ensure that the prospective buyer is able to ascertain all the facts about a slave, so that he is able to discover any diseases or defects he may have; whether he is likely to try to run away or loiter about aimlessly; or whether the slave is free from any legal liability for a claim for damages. Those who sell slaves must state the origin of birth of each slave they offer for sale. You should pay particular heed to this. For the origin of a slave frequently determines whether or not they will become a good slave, with some tribes having a far better reputation than others. One would not, for instance, consider using a nasty little Briton as a personal servant, given their rough manners and demeanour. By contrast, young Egyptian boys make for excellent pets.

Opinions differ as to what is the best source for slaves. One thing all agree about, however, is that it is abhorrent to use fellow Roman citizens as slaves, as might otherwise happen if they have perhaps fallen into heavy debt. Instead, these poor cases should be sold abroad so they should not create unease among their owners, who would otherwise have to give instructions for menial tasks to those who had once been part of the proudest race of people in the world. For it is wrong that those who have been born as free Romans should end up in servitude. Even the German barbarians refuse to use their own people in this way. You may be surprised to learn that this dour race are fanatical gamblers, to such an extent that they will risk everything, including their freedom, to win one last throw of the dice. If they lose they will submit to being led away in chains. They claim it is because their honour is at stake but to me it seems like simple obstinacy. But the winner will always ensure that he sells such an enslaved free man abroad, in order that they should not on a daily basis have to feel ashamed at having caused such a downfall by seeing the loser working in their neighbourhood.

The great philosopher Seneca thought that home-bred slaves were best because they knew no other life and so were less likely to champ at the bit, as it were. Cicero's friend Atticus was so fussy that he would only use home-breds for domestic slaves. In his view, home-born slaves are far more likely to remain loyal to their master, seeing him almost as a father, nor do they bear any grudge against him for their enslavement. The problem with this is, as we shall see, that breeding slaves is both expensive and time-consuming.

And, in any case, there are many who argue that a new slave is like wet clay, capable of being moulded into whatever shape the master wishes. Like puppies, they can be trained quickly to perform their tasks in a certain fashion, rather than be brought up over long years to achieve the same end. Newly captured barbarians will obviously need to be broken in. And when buying one, it is important to remember that it will take them some time to grow accustomed to their new, much reduced station in life. We should show them some leniency in these early days and even some sympathy. For how can we not pity someone who tries to hold on to some vestige of his former status and is less than enthusiastic at performing the sordid tasks we assign to him? Do not punish him too hard if he has grown unfit during transportation and imprisonment and is unable to keep up with your horse on foot. Or if he is not used to having to be on his toes all day, awaiting his master's call, and keeps falling asleep. Similarly, second-hand slaves cannot be expected to adapt to their new roles seamlessly. If they have come from an easy life in Rome, with all the holidays and gentle household jobs that entails, then they are going to find life in the country exhausting.

One point of special caution is not to buy too many slaves from the same background or nationality. While it may seem superficially appealing to have slaves who are able to work together and co-operate easily, on account of the fact that they speak the same language, this can generate great problems. At best, the slaves will conspire among themselves to work lazily, sit about chatting, and steal from you; at worst, they will argue, fight and plot to escape or even murder you. It is far better to source your slaves from a range of nationalities. Then they will be unable to converse with each other. Not only will this prevent servile collusion in shirking their work, but it will also force them to acquire the rudiments of Latin. This will in time enable you to issue orders to them more freely and for you to overhear the contents of their conversations and gossip.

Be very careful about buying slaves who have been snatched in raids by pirates. I once bought one by mistake – the dealer misled me as to how he had acquired him – and once he had learnt some Latin, the fellow insisted to me that he was in reality a free man. He claimed that he came from the town of Mothone on the Adriatic Sea, where one day a number of ships had put in pretending to be traders from the east. They agreed to buy wine from the town at the price which the Mothonians had asked for, and even sold them some of their own merchandise of spices. The following day, more people came into the town from the surrounding area since they had heard that there were opportunities for trade and for buying exotic oriental items. Eventually, the quayside was brimming with men and women trying to sell them wine and barter goods from them in return. But as the wine was being carted down to the harbour, the pirates, for that in truth is what they were, suddenly grabbed as many of the men and women as they could and forcibly drove them on to their ships, before sailing off and leaving the town denuded of people. Naturally, I assumed he was telling a lie to win his freedom falsely but he persisted and even persuaded a magistrate to hear his case, although it was kicked out for lack of evidence. In the end I was forced to sell him at a significant loss so that I would not have to put up with his incessant grumbling.

The price you should be prepared to pay for a slave will obviously vary according to the quality of the merchandise. Be aware that slaves are not cheap. On average you should expect to pay 1,000 sesterces for a healthy adult male, who is somewhere between fifteen and forty years of age. A comparable woman will cost a little less, say 800. Given that a poor man can probably feed a family of four for little more than 500 sesterces a year, it will be clear to you what a considerable investment slaves represent. Older and younger slaves will be a similar price, with the over-forties fetching about 800, and a youth between the ages of eight and fifteen the same. Those of extreme old age or youth, the over-sixties and children below the age of eight, will be cheaper, costing perhaps 400 sesterces. Bear in mind that prices will be far higher if the slave has been trained in a skill, such as reading, accounting or barbering.

Of course, the sky is the limit if your funds allow. There have been many examples of the wealthy paying colossal sums for exceptional specimens, who might reflect favourably on the status of their owner. Mark Antony, for example, was sold two particularly attractive twin slaves by the dealer Toranius. He is reputed to have paid 200,000 sesterces. But it turned out to be a con because one had actually been born in Asia and the other north of the Alps, a fact that emerged because they spoke with such different accents. When a furious Mark Antony confronted Toranius, the quick-witted dealer replied that this was the real reason he had demanded such a high price: that there was nothing special about twin brothers looking alike, but to find such similarity in two boys from different races was unique and priceless. Mark Antony was so surprised that, even though he had been in a rage, he now believed that these 'twins' were the finest possessions he owned and duly reflected his great status as co-ruler of Rome with Octavian.

I might add that the highest 'normal' price I have been able to discover that has been paid for a slave was when Marcus Scaurus offered 750,000 sesterces for the grammarian Daphnis, who was being sold by Attius of Pisaurum. Naturally, this figure has been greatly exceeded by famous slave-actors buying their freedom out of their colossal earnings. Long ago, the actor Roscius supposedly earnt 500,000 a year, so he must have paid much more to get himself freed. There have also been some special cases. One of Nero's slaves, who ran his military campaign against Tiridates in Armenia, was sold his freedom in return for the plunder, which amounted to some 13 million sesterces. And so, too, when Lutorius Priscus bought the eunuch Paezon from the emperor Tiberius's henchman Sejanus for 50 million sesterces. The price was given to gratify his lust and to advertise his wealth not because the slave was somehow worth it. It is a sign of how terrible and anxious that period was, under Sejanus's wicked influence, that the people were too preoccupied to put a stop to a bargain of so scandalous a nature.

It is worth giving some thought as to the type of character that a slave you are thinking of buying possesses. Does he seem weak-willed or reckless? The types best suited for work are those who are neither extremely cowardly nor extremely brave, since both of these are likely to cause trouble. Those who are too easily cowed will not persevere with their work, while those who have too much courage are difficult to control. On the other hand, in some positions, particularly when it comes to choosing domestic servants, it is useful to seek out those who are deferential and unassertive. Household slaves should be like mice – quiet, timid, but always scurrying busily around. Of course, you should beware those who are merely putting on such attributes for the sake of a quiet life. Many slaves act tamely in order to be entrusted with some gentle household occupation, such as being a waiter at table, which gives them opportunities for relaxation between meals and for eating the fine leftovers from our plates.

When it comes to buying slaves, let the buyer beware! If you perchance see a slave in whom you are interested you must be sure to examine him or her closely. Just as you would take the cover from a horse you intended to buy so that you might better be able to look at its physique and spot any existing or potential weaknesses, so you should have the slave dealer make the slave undress. Dealers are the most untrustworthy sort and often they will seek to conceal defects with clothing. They will use a long tunic to hide knock knees. Or brightly coloured clothes to distract from weak and puny arms. Check that male slaves have both their testicles intact, since you will likely want to breed from them. In other words, you must be sure to prod and poke to make sure you reveal the truth of the physical specimen in front of you.

Slave dealers are a most unscrupulous bunch and are to be guarded against at all costs. Their only interest is in generating as large a profit as possible, which they will seek to achieve by all kinds of trickery. Dealers in eunuchs are the worst since they will even mutilate their possessions in contravention of nature's intentions to increase their value. Many slaves are damaged in transit to the marketplace, suffering weight-loss or injury from the chafing of chains. Beware some of the dealers' tricks to conceal these defects. For emaciated slaves they apply resin from the terebinth tree to relax the skin so that they can be easily fattened up again. Or they will apply depilatories made of blood, gall and tuna liver to remove adolescent males' hair and make them look younger. Or they mix root of hyacinth with sweet wine and feed it to adolescents to slow the signs of puberty and the onset of sexual development. Other frauds include using dye to add colour to the pale cheeks of an ailing slave, or dressing them with finery to cover barely healed old wounds and scars.

Ask questions. Do not take anything the dealer says at face value. Quiz him about the slave's character. If the slave is female make sure he declares whether she is incapable of bearing children. Find out if she has ever given birth to stillborn infants, or whether she menstruates regularly. Discover whether the slave has ever committed a capital offence, tried to run away, or been condemned to fight the beasts in the arena. All of these facts display the sort of character that you could well do without in your household. Beware the clever slave, unless you are looking to train them as a letter-writer or reader. For the clever slave is a troublesome slave in any other position. But enquire also about moral defects: does the slave have a gambling habit, is he prone to drink too much if given the opportunity, does he prefer the company of other male slaves?

Avoid slaves who appear melancholy. Being a slave is hardly the most enviable job and those with a depressive disposition will find it turns their mood black. Indeed, it is one of the bugbears of slave-ownership that we have to rely on individuals who frequently break down in tears or even attempt suicide. The law states that sellers are obliged to reveal to prospective buyers if a slave has tried to kill himself but we cannot always be sure that the truth is being told so would do well to trust our instincts. This is a more common problem than you might realise. For, as the proverbs say, 'It is beautiful to die instead of being degraded as a slave'; and 'If you don't like being a slave, you will be miserable; but you won't stop being a slave.'

Once you have carefully selected your slave and agreed a price, make sure you get a contract. In accordance with our contract law, the vendor should put up a guarantor to stand surety for him should the buyer be dissatisfied in some justifiable way. The contract will state your name and position, the name of the slave, or any other name he may have, his race, the price, the name of the vendor, the name of his guarantor, the date, and the place where the contract has been drawn up. Note that in the purchase of slaves, it is customary for the slave's own possessions, including any money he has managed to save, to go with the slave, unless it is expressly stated otherwise.

Make sure you have a written guarantee from the dealer as to the slave's healthiness. Be sure to understand what the guarantee is protection against: matters such as disease, a tendency to run away and gambling habits must be declared; defects such as laziness and having bad breath need not be. It is not always clear what healthy means. Is a slave whose tongue has been cut out healthy? In fact there are as many possible minor defects in slaves as there are slaves. I've had them all: bed-wetters, epileptics, missing toes, stammerers, thieves. We all know what a bad slave is: he is fickle, lazy, slow, late, greedy, obstinate, ugly, pot-bellied and squint-eyed, he slouches and shrugs his shoulders as he speaks. By contrast we all know what a good slave is: loyal, hard-working and vigilant. The problem is that it is often very difficult to tell them apart when they have been brushed up by the slave dealers.

Once purchased you will also have to consider what work you are going to put your slave to doing. There is a multitude of possible tasks that can await him. Slaves divide broadly into two types: rural and urban. Those employed in the countryside can be taught the crafts of the ploughman, the pruner, the water-carrier, the potter, the sweeper and so on. The slave women can be assigned to such roles as clothes-folder, furniture-polisher, wool-weigher or masseuse. Those who are set to work in the urban household also need to be matched to particular tasks. Beauty, for example, is best suited for serving at table. If you are wealthy, you will expect to have a retinue of slaves, all filling different positions within the household. There must be litter-bearers, a secretary to read your letters to you aloud, and write your replies. Others should be set to provide gentle musical accompaniment at mealtimes, or employed as doorkeepers, concubines, timekeepers and messengers.

Female slaves can be kept for household tasks and

breeding. The disreputable, of course, buy them to work as prostitutes in brothels. These days many Roman mothers do not wish to perform the difficult task of nursing their own children and prefer to leave it to slave wet-nurses. Here, choosing the right nurse is especially important, since this is often the woman whom your child will first call 'mummy'. When it comes to babysitting my children, then, I like to employ slave children whom I have fathered with my own slave women. The slaves who are closest to you, as their master, are those who looked after you when you were young. My old childhood-tutor, Felix, used to take me to school every morning, kept me safe from any trouble and helped in everything from getting dressed to playing at gladiators. Of course he had been given the job because he was useless for anything else. As the great Athenian statesman Pericles said when he saw a slave fall from a tree and break his leg: 'He's just become a tutor.'

Many of these tutors are actually highly educated. You should decide whether you want a thoroughly uneducated helper for your boys, like Felix, or a properly educated slave who can help them develop into the great orators you would like them to be. The worst thing is to use a slave who has a little learning but becomes convinced of his own genius. They constantly interfere with the child's proper education and sometimes even brutally impose their own stupidity on the children. This is particularly important because these tutors can easily infect their charges with their own vices. Even Alexander the Great is reputed to have been permanently afflicted with the vices of his tutor Leonidas.

Beware of ostentation. There is nothing more vulgar than some social parvenu employing a whole host of completely unnecessary slaves to carry out the most worthless tasks simply as a means to advertise their master's excessive wealth. One wealthy freedman I know had a nomenclator, a name-caller, whose function was to remind their master of the names of the people he met. How insulting for his guests to have their name prompted by some slave. What is even worse is when people give this job to some old retainer who is good for no kind of productive work and whose brain is addled by age. They make constant mistakes and cause great embarrassment to all. Perhaps the most ridiculous use of slaves in this manner was made by a very rich man called Calvisius Sabinus. He inherited a huge estate, but was uneducated and his memory was so bad that he could not even remember the names of the heroes in Homer's epics. Wanting to appear as an educated man, and somehow therefore deserving of his fortune, he bought some clever slaves at great expense and set them to memorising the great works of literature. One was to memorise the whole of Homer off by heart, another Hesiod, and nine others were to learn by rote the nine lyric poets. It took great training for them to be able to read well enough to achieve this. But once he had this literary slave gang in place he started to pester his dinner guests, continually asking them for some lines of poetry for his crew to quote. Sabinus claimed that these slaves had cost him a fortune. The same number of bookcases would have been cheaper.

Of course, not all slaves are owned by such silly private individuals. The state also employs many public slaves to do such things as keep reliable accounts and maintain the roads. These can make a sound investment if you are looking to acquire second-hand slaves since they have not been worked overly hard and are often delighted to be given the chance to work in the dynamic atmosphere of the private household, even if this means a decline in status. But even with the state's slaves great care does need to be exercised. When the emperor Trajan sent Pliny to Bithynia as governor to investigate alleged corruption, he discovered that convicted criminals who had evaded their punishment were being employed as public slaves. They were even being paid an annual stipend, like most public slaves, and had been in post for long periods of time. Indeed many were by then quite old and were, by all accounts, now leading virtuous lives. Naturally the emperor demanded that these criminals should suffer their proper punishment, unless it was long in the past, in which case they should be allocated to those jobs which were as good as punishments, such as working in the public baths or cleaning the sewers.

With regard to the number of slaves you might have to buy, the great Cato says we should, in the matter of rural slaves, base the calculation on the size of the estate and the type of crops to be grown. Writing about olive groves and vineyards, he gives two formulae. The first is one in which he shows how an olive grove of 60 hectares should be equipped. For a farm of this size, he says that the following thirteen slaves should be kept: an overseer, a housekeeper, five labourers, three teamsters, one muleteer, one swineherd and one shepherd. The second formula he gives is for a vineyard of 25 hectares, on which he says should be kept the following fifteen slaves: an overseer, a housekeeper, ten labourers, a teamster, a muleteer and a swineherd. Others state that one man is enough for 2 hectares, and that he should be able to dig over that area in forty-five days, when allowing for the usual inconveniences such as illness, bad weather and idleness. But personally I think these rules are too vague. Cato should have stated his formula in such a way that we can add or subtract from the number proportionately according to whether the farm is larger or smaller. Further, he should have kept the overseer and the housekeeper outside of the number of slaves that is required. For if you cultivate less than 60 hectares of olives you cannot get along with less than one overseer.

The number of herdsmen is determined differently, with various calculations being popular. My own practice is to have a herdsman to every 80 to 100 wool-bearing sheep. If flocks of sheep are very large (and some people have as many as 1,000) you can decrease the number of shepherds more easily than you can in smaller flocks. My own flocks contain 700. Two men are needed for a herd of 50 mares, and each of these should certainly have for his use a mare that has been broken in. Rich landlords generally entrust all these functions of a great estate to members of their own household. If towns or villages are too far from their farm, they make sure that they have some blacksmiths on the estate as well as other essential craftsmen, so that the slaves on the farm won't have to leave off working and idle about on work days as if they were on holiday, instead of making the farm more profitable by getting on with their tasks.

Oh how different were things in the great days of our forefathers! There was none of this discussion of how best to employ our great swathes of slaves. Back then they lived simply, with perhaps a single slave who took their meals in common with the master. Now we even have to lock up our pantries to protect the household's food and wine from being stolen by the legions of household slaves, that great crowd of outsiders we have let inside our homes. Indeed there are so many of them that we even need a slave just to remind us of the names of our slaves!

What has happened to old-fashioned self-sufficiency? Why do we need to own great retinues of slaves just to show off how rich we are? Look at the heavens and you will see that the gods are naked; they give everything and keep nothing for themselves. Then look at the earth and see the rapacious individuals who gather round themselves all manner of slaves to boost their public image. Was Pompey's freedman Demetrius, who felt no shame at being richer than Pompey, also happier? Every day he used to go through the list of slaves he owned as though he were an army commander. He should have considered himself well off if he had just two under-slaves and more spacious sleeping quarters. Diogenes had just one slave who ran away from him, and when he was told where he was, he didn't think it worthwhile to bring him back. 'It would be dishonourable,' he said, 'if my slave Manes could survive without Diogenes, but Diogenes could not survive without Manes.' I think that what he meant was this: 'Now that wretched slave has run away, I've got my freedom back!'

Slaves are nothing but an expense. You have to look after the appetites of all those greedy creatures. You have to buy them clothes. You have to keep a watch on all those thieving hands ever ready to steal things. You have to use people who also detest us. How much happier is the man whose only obligation is to someone whom he can easily deny – himself!

But how can we fight the riches that fate has sent us? Perhaps we shall just have to accept that it is written in the stars that we Romans are destined to rule the world. We cannot avoid owning slaves. At the very least you should display your ambivalence about owning slaves in the names that you chose for them. Pick a cheerful name or one that means something to you, such as the place where you bought him, or a name imbued with some dry humour to show that you do not take seriously the benefits that fortune has chosen to send your way. For example, I once bought a slave, at no inconsiderable cost, who on his journey to my urban villa fell and broke his arm. I called him Lucky.

·· COMMENTARY ··

Most of the details regarding the purchase of slaves come from the urban environment where a master was generally buying a small number of slaves. The fact that these slaves lived under the same roof as the master and were used to provide personal services to him and his family means that it was likely that great care was taken over their selection. It was probably different in the country. Particularly in large estates, such detailed examinations may not have been the norm and it probably fell to the estate manager to buy the slaves. Obviously, the size of a master's household and estates will have dictated the degree of his personal involvement in making slave purchases.

The availability of slaves will have affected the care that buyers took in their selections. In periods after great Roman military victories, when the supply of new slaves was plentiful, prices can be expected to have fallen and buyers probably relaxed their watchfulness.

A freeborn Roman citizen could not legally forfeit his or her legal status without consent. But it was a sad fact of social life in the Roman world that many freeborn children were abandoned by their parents who either could not afford to bring them up or simply did not want to. Those who did not die of exposure to the elements or from being eaten by dogs could be picked up by slave dealers and surrogate parents and raised as foundlings. These children effectively became the slaves of their new guardians. Even though it was a common mechanism in theatrical plots for such abandoned children to be rediscovered by their real parents, it is safe to assume that this was a rare occurrence.

It is actually unclear whether the Romans actively bred their slaves. Slave reproduction happened naturally, given that they were often allowed to form relationships. The master seems to have been expected to give his approval for such partnerships, but the extent of his involvement in pairing slaves off is unknown. If the master was consulted, it is reasonable to assume that he would have wanted to prevent an alliance between two troublesome slaves, but that is a long way from saying that he sought to manage his slave stock by selecting well-built and healthy slaves as partners for each other. Masters also indulged in sexual activity with their slaves, which, if female slaves were involved, also resulted in servile pregnancies. These offspring were legally slaves, even though the master was the father.

Prices for slaves need to be treated with caution. They are estimates based on a small body of surviving examples. Nominal prices rose during the later empire because of inflation but it is unclear whether prices increased in real terms. It is certainly not possible to see any decline in the total slave population of the later empire, either as a result of possible economic decline or Christianity's greater influence. Records of the dramatically high prices of slaves such as Mark Antony's 'twins' have survived because of their extreme nature. It is impossible to draw any conclusions about more average prices from this. What can be concluded about prices more generally is that they were both high and varied. It cost about 500 sesterces per year to feed a family of four with a simple grain diet. Obviously, once a greater variety of foodstuffs and other living costs such as rent and clothing are taken into account, that figure will rise much higher. If we take 1,000 sesterces as a reasonable guess, even allowing for the fact that this will have varied significantly from place to place and from year to year, then the prices given by Marcus can obviously be seen to be very high. They are certainly well above the means of the poor or maybe even 'average' Roman. A slave would also have represented a substantial investment for an artisan. It shows how the large retinues of slaves maintained by the rich had little to do with economics and lots to do with conspicuous consumption.

Despite the huge number of slaves kept in Italy, many Roman texts seem to have had moral problems with the use of slaves. It is sometimes very difficult to square this conflict. How did the Romans use so many slaves but think it was morally wrong to do so? We need to recognise the rhetorical element of so many Roman sources, particularly from writers such as Seneca, who provides a number of important texts related to slavery. The decline of Rome from its purity of old was a literary motif. It was how the Romans assuaged their guilt at consuming so much, whether it was in the form of food in feasts or people as slaves.

Digest 21.1 gives details of the *Edict of the Curule Aediles*, which governed the sale of slaves and lists the details of defects that had to be revealed. On foundlings, see for example Pliny the Younger *Letters* 10.65 and 66. Aulus Gellius *Attic Nights* 20.1 describes how from the fourth century BC Rome did not allow its citizens to sell themselves as slaves to pay back debts. Earlier, it had been possible, but such slaves had to be sold across the Tiber, which was at that time outside Roman territory. On Germans as fanatical dice-players see Tacitus *Germania* 24. The pirate raid on Mothone is to be found at Pausanias 4.35.6. The description of the capture of a small city is based on the Roman capture of Palermo in 259 BC described in Diodorus Siculus 23.18. Prices are based on the 5 million sesterces raised by Augustus's 2 per cent sales tax on slaves and by the relative pricing of wheat and slaves in Diocletian's *Edict on Maximum Prices*. I have given prices in sesterces at about the time of Augustus. For extreme prices see Pliny the Elder *Natural History* 7.40; see the same source, 7.12, for Mark Antony's twins; and 7.39 for the actors, Nero and Paezon. On pitying new slaves who find their altered status difficult see Seneca *On Anger* 3.29. The proverbs can be found in Publius Syrus nos. 489 and 616. The story of Calvisius Sabinus training his slaves to memorise Homer is in Seneca *Letters* 27. On childhood tutors see Quintilian *Institutes of Oratory* 1.1. The account of Pliny the Younger writing to the emperor Trajan about criminals being used as public slaves is in his *Letters* 10.31 and 32. 'Lucky' (Felix) was a common slave name.

CHAPTER II

GETTING THE BEST FROM YOUR SLAVES

S O YOU HAVE BOUGHT your slaves. How now do you manage them in such a way that they will work hard for you? Many a new slave owner has fallen into the trap of thinking that the whip alone is enough. Those of us whose families have possessed slaves for generations know that such treatment will soon wear a slave out. If you try to force your slaves beyond the limits of reasonable service, you will end up making them surly and unmanageable. Slaves like this are a vexation and a curse. Cruelty ends up hurting the master most. It might do for the mines but not on your farm estates, let alone in your household. Instead, you must realise that as a master you have an obligation to treat your slaves properly, and if you do that, then you can expect not only that they will do their jobs diligently but that they will remain fit to do so for many years to come.

It is incumbent on the higher orders in society to behave justly towards even the lowest kinds of people. There are none who are lower than the slaves. But we should treat them in the same way that we do hired workmen. That is to say, we should insist that they work properly but that we should treat them fairly in return. This is despite the fact that slaves are, of course, no more than tools. A hired workman is a man. But a slave is a tool that is used to work the land or provide some other service. A slave just happens to be a tool that can speak. It is this faculty of speech that ranks him above the cattle and other farm animals. But you as a master and slave owner are at the top of society and it is right that you act in a moral and just manner at all times, even to those who do not deserve it.

The first step you must take to ensure that your slaves behave well and work hard has already been done: you have bought good slaves. The next step is training them. It is clear to everyone that the way in which you bring up your children is reflected in their individual character. In the same way, it is essential that you educate and train your slaves properly for the roles that you wish to assign to them. This is why it is often best and easiest to buy slaves who are new to servitude. I mentioned that one friend of mine always buys prisoners of war who are still young enough to be trained, in the way that foals are so much more biddable than mangy old nags.

Training can begin immediately. Some foolishly believe that it is possible to reason with a slave. They think that slaves can be made more likely to obey you simply by explaining to them the advantages of doing so. But in fact slaves need to be trained as you would a wild beast if obedience is to be instilled. Again, this is not a simple matter of the whip. You will get the best results by giving them as much food as they want. Praise them generously, especially those who are clearly ambitious and so are likely to be more motivated by praise. Make sure that you compel them to forget their old gods and start to worship at the household shrine. Once they realise that it is our pantheon of gods that has made us great, they will be far more likely to accept the justness of their low position.

Once trained, give slaves enough food for them to do their jobs, but not so much as to make them lazy. Those slaves who are performing manual labour should receive more generous rations than those who are performing light domestic duties. Slaves need fuel to work efficiently and cannot be expected to give good service on an empty belly. I always make a point of checking the slaves' rations personally whenever I visit my estates. This ensures that the cooks are not cheating by keeping some of the supplies aside for their own profit. It also shows the slaves that you are taking an interest in their welfare, which will boost their morale and make them work harder. For there are three things that slaves think about: food, work and punishment. If you give them food to eat but no work to do, it will make them lazy and insolent. If you give them work and punishment without food it quickly weakens them in the same way as violent attacks do. By far the best course is to give them work to do together with sufficient food. You cannot manage people without rewarding them, and food is a slave's reward. Slaves are just like normal people in that they perform badly if good behaviour brings no benefits and there are no punishments for failure.

Keep a close eye, therefore, on your slaves' behaviour and allocate your food accordingly. Privileges should be granted in accordance with how well they have been deserved. Food makes a good bonus for pleasing performance. I like to reward domestic slaves with the leftovers from my dinners when they have served well. In the country, I give slaves free time to have the opportunity to keep their own chickens and pigs and tend their own kitchen gardens, or go foraging in the woods for berries and the like. Or I will give them extra rations of the hard cheese made in Luna in Etruria. I will also give them a little extra wine vinegar, but be very careful here. Drinking wine makes even free men behave insolently, so it should be obvious that extra wine should be given to slaves only rarely and under supervision.

In all our dealings with the victuals of slaves we must act like a doctor when he issues his prescriptions. Great care must be made to ensure that each slave gets both what is just and what is suitable for his lowly position. Slave food should be functional not luxurious. I recommend a basic diet of rough bread, salt, grapes, olive oil, olive mash and dried fruit. This can be supplemented with small performance bonuses as described above. You will find the following guides useful:

Rations for slaves:

30 kg of wheat per month in winter for slaves in chain gangs.

35 kg of wheat per month in summer to allow for the harder work of sowing, weeding and harvesting crops.

Increase rations when slaves begin to work the vines, and reduce them when the figs ripen. Do not cut them back as much as that cheapskate Cato advises in his manual unless you wish to wear your slaves out with hunger.

20 kg of wheat per month for the overseer, the housekeeper, the foremen, and shepherds, to allow for their lighter load.

Recipe for slave wine rations:

Put in a wooden barrel ten parts of crushed grapes and two parts of very pungent vinegar. Add two parts of boiled wine and fifty of sweet water. With a paddle mix all these three times a day for five days. Add one forty-eighth of seawater drawn some time earlier. Place a lid on the barrel and let it ferment for ten days.

Obviously this is not the finest Falernian! But it should last for about three months and if there is any left after then it will make excellent, very sharp vinegar.

Olives for slaves:

Store all the windfall olives you can. Add the small olives from mature olive trees, which will yield very little oil. Issue these olives sparingly to the slaves to make them last as long as possible. When they are used up, give the slaves fish-pickle and vinegar. Give slaves a pint of oil a month. Also give them half a pound of salt each per month.

During the day, slaves should eat their lunch sitting separately to avoid time-wasting and idle chatting. But in the evenings they should be allowed to eat together. For we would be too hard if we did not permit them some socialising.

Clothes should also be given out according to how well they are deserved. Those slaves who have worked hard should be rewarded with better quality shoes and tunics, whereas those who have shirked their responsibilities must realise that they face the consequences of their idleness in all aspects of their life. As a standard rule, I give each farm slave a one-metre-long tunic and a coarse blanket every other year. When you issue the tunic or the blanket, make sure that you make them hand in their old ones so that your female slaves can make patchwork from them. A stout pair of wooden shoes should be issued every other year. In all matters of clothing you should think about usefulness rather then appearance. To keep the slave protected against wind, cold and rain, give them long-sleeved leather tunics, extra patchwork clothes, or hooded cloaks. If you do this then there is no weather so bad that some work cannot be done outside.

Your slaves need adequate shelter to sleep in. House your domestic slaves in small bedrooms or storage rooms, and provide an old mattress for them to lie on and an old cloak to use as a blanket. In the country, you will almost certainly find room among the rafters of some building to use as sleeping quarters for the slaves. If it is large enough, and the risk of fire is low, then you may well find the rafters in the kitchen can provide a cosy area all year round. The worst thing for a farm is to be worked by slaves housed in a kind of underground prison block, for anything that is done by men who have no hope is done badly.

It is a sad fact that today, wherever you travel in the empire, you see the land being worked by slaves instead of the yeomen of old who made Rome great. These days, farms are trod by feet in chains, by hands which have been punished, by faces which have been branded. Mother Earth is not so stupid that she doesn't notice that proud and free peasants have been swapped for insolent and lazy slaves. It is not surprising that we do not get the same profits from farms worked by slaves as we used to get from the labour of Roman citizens. The fundamental problem is that the slave has no incentive to work hard. He gets fed whatever the farm produces. But there are some precautions you can undertake to try to minimise this shortfall and force or bribe the slave into working more productively.

The first, which I have already mentioned but cannot emphasise enough, is to reward hard work. It is very demoralising for good slaves if they see that they are doing all the hard work, but that the lazy slaves get just as much food as they do. It is also essential that each slave should have a clearly defined long-term goal. If you are so minded, this can be for them to win their freedom. You will find it both fair and beneficial to offer freedom as a long-term bonus for loyalty and hard work. If the slave believes that the goal is attainable then he will work diligently towards it. Allowing your slaves to have children provides them with another incentive to work hard. If they do they will enjoy the fruits and pleasures of an improved family life. But if they displease you, then the children can be sold off to another owner as a punishment. If you organise occasional sacrifices and holidays as a reward for the hardest workers then you will also make it more likely that the work will get done well.

The second is to have clear job roles. This generates clear accountability and ensures hard work, since slaves knows that if a certain piece of work is not carried out then the blame can clearly be laid at the feet of one of them. If, on the other hand, everyone does the same thing, none of the slaves will think that any job is his own responsibility. If an individual works hard then all will benefit, rather than him specifically, whereas if they all slack off then it is impossible to identify who was most responsible. That is why ploughmen must be kept distinct from vineyard workers and shepherds distinct from ordinary labourers.

As part of this specialisation, each slave must be encouraged to take personal responsibility for the care and upkeep of his tools. He must be urged to store them away from the rain, clean and oil them and not leave them lying around. The cost of replacing such tools is in itself expensive but it also means that many days' labour are lost from having slaves sitting about without the tools to work. Giving them their own tools and punishing those who fail in this duty will help reduce such losses markedly.

There is a final benefit to this dividing of the roles among your slaves: the estate will become self-sufficient. For every task you will have a slave. So if you need a shearer you will have one, a barber, you will have one, a blacksmith, you will have one. No longer will you have to hire in the costly services of outside contractors.

Gang labour makes slaves work faster, harder and better. You should form them into groups of about ten. This is a particularly easy number of men to keep watch over. Larger gangs can be difficult for an overseer to control on his own. So, on your estate, you should assign these groups to different sections of it, and the work should be distributed in such a way that the men will not be on their own or in pairs, since they cannot be supervised properly if they are scattered all over the place. The other problem with larger groups is that the individuals within the group will not feel that the work has anything to do with them personally. It all gets lost in the crowd. But a gang of the right size has the effect of making individuals compete with each other, and also identifies the shirkers. Jobs always become more interesting when there is an element of competition. It will also mean that no one will complain when those who don't pull their weight are punished for it.

Take care to assign each slave to the kind of work most suitable to his or her physical or mental attributes. Herdsmen, for example, should be diligent and very thrifty. These two qualities are more important for this role than stature or physical strength, since it requires concentration and skill. When it comes to ploughmen, intelligence, though necessary, is still not sufficient. You need a slave with a big voice that will make him scary to the cattle. Yet he should also be gentle, because otherwise he will treat your cattle cruelly and they will neither obey his commands nor will they last long before they get worn out by the hardship and the torment of his lash.

When it comes to shepherds, you should again bear in mind that strength and height are of no use in that job. Make your taller slaves ploughmen because there is no job on the farm that is less tiring to a tall man than ploughing. This is because when ploughing a field the slave stands upright and rests his weight on the plough handle. When it comes to general labourers and field workers, slaves can be any size or shape you want. All they need is to be able to cope with hard work. Slaves who you assign to work in the vineyards should be broad-shouldered and muscular. These physical types are well suited to digging and pruning. It also matters less if they are dishonest because vineyard slaves work together in groups, so are easily supervised. It is also the case that dishonest slaves tend to be the cleverer ones, which is a benefit when it comes to tending vines since they need strong and intelligent care. This is why you so often see vineyards being looked after by slaves in chains. Mind you, an honest man of equal intelligence will always perform better than a thief.

Don't think that slaves are always best for farming your estates. It is definitely better to work unhealthy land with hired labourers than with slaves since it requires greater dedication and effort. It is also probably better to use free men to carry out the more important agricultural tasks, such as bringing in the grape harvest. Some special problems arise from using slaves as herdsmen and shepherds. This is a particularly difficult and unpopular job, not only because the herdsmen are exposed to the elements but because they also face the risk of being

attacked by bandits and wild beasts. It is a lonely existence too, with long periods away from human contact,
from sociability and from the household. It is best to
leave such troublesome jobs to poor free men who need
the money and so can be relied upon to do a decent job.

If you do use slaves as herdsmen you must realise that
it is almost impossible to supervise them. They are likely
to cause problems wherever they go, either by stealing
things or getting into fights. You must also realise that
you need to use different kinds of physical specimens
for different kinds of herding. Use older slaves for larger
animals, but assign small boys to the small animals. Those
who go out with the cattle along the trails in the hills
and pastures must be stronger than those who tend beasts
back at the farm. That is of course why you see young
men out in the pastures when boys and even young slave
girls can cope with looking after the animals on the farm
itself.

Herdsmen must be expected to spend the whole
day with their flocks. They should also spend the whole
night with them. The herdsmen should all report to a
Head Herdsman, who should be older and more experienced than the others in order to command respect. But
he must not be so old that he cannot cope with hard
work. Not many old men can put up with the hardships
of the cattle trail, when they have to travel along steep
and rugged mountainsides, especially if they are herding
goats.

Select men who have powerful physiques, are quick
and agile, who are well coordinated, and are able to
defend the flock from wild beasts or rustlers. They need

to be strong enough to lift up loads on to the backs of the pack animals, are good at sprinting and at hitting things with their slingshots. I find some races are useless as herdsmen. Bastulans and Turdulans are both no good, but Gauls are particularly good at it, especially with beasts of burden. As discussed, in terms of the number of herdsmen you employ, I would have one for every 80 to 100 sheep, and two for every 50 mares.

The Head Herdsman must make sure that all the supplies the flock and the herdsmen need are available to them, above all the men's food and the animals' veterinary supplies. The Head Herdsman should also be able to write so that he can keep records for you to inspect. This will also enable him to write down the directions for treating the illnesses that commonly attack animals and humans, so that he can help the sick when they are away in the grazing pastures and far from the aid of any physician.

Cato thought that slaves should either be working or that they should be asleep. He was actually quite happy to have slaves who slept a lot because he thought that they were easier to control than those who had a lot of energy. He also believed that those slaves who liked to sleep were more likely to be respectful towards their master. He never allowed domestic slaves to leave the confines of his own household unless explicitly sent on an errand by him or his wife. Even then they were not allowed to converse with others in case this encouraged them to idle. He thought that sexual appetite was what made slaves most difficult to control and so he used to charge them a fixed price to get together with the female slaves. But he would not allow them any kind of permanent relationship. In my view this is no way to run a household. Humanity, even when it comes in the form of a miserable slave, still demands some basic justice.

Some see sick and old slaves as unproductive and useless. Cato advises us that they should be thrown away like rubbish. His attitude was that slaves should be bought cheap, worked hard and then left to die. He would simply not feed them once they were no longer useful. I, and most slave owners I know, consider his advice to be too cruel and heartless. Frankly, he was more worried about his sick fish than he was about his ill slaves and it is in any case now illegal to dump them. Personally, I think that an owner who treats his slaves like mules and then gets rid of them when they get old is wrong because he sees no bond between an owner and his slaves.

We owners have responsibilities towards our dependants. It will not always be in our financial interest to keep on a sick slave. But we can at least give them a chance to recover and lighten their load while they do so. And we can find some gentle jobs for the old slaves to perform, which enables them to contribute to the household. It is, after all, quite rare that slaves live into old age given the demands that are placed upon them. I use them as doorkeepers, or as bag-carriers for my sons when they go to school.

As an aside, let me tell you of an embarrassing incident I had with an old doorkeeper when visiting an old friend's villa. I went up to the entrance where a decrepit slave was keeping watch. 'Where on earth did you get hold of him?' I asked my friend. 'What possessed you to steal a corpse from a graveyard to guard the door?' But my friend said to me, 'Don't you recognise him, Marcus? It's Felicio. We used to play together when we were children during the Saturnalia. He was the son of my father's manager, Philositus, and we were all playmates.' I had no idea what he was talking about. 'You're completely mad!' I told my friend. 'How could this toothless old crone have been a contemporary of ours?' My friend's look said it all! It is true that we have all been wearied by the passing years, but the life of a slave had certainly taken its toll on Felicio. But then I'm surprised my friend remembered him at all. He was, after all, only a slave boy.

While I am on the subject of age, I should say that when it comes to very young slaves I am all in favour of getting them working as soon as possible, certainly by the age of five. There is always something useful they can do, whether it is tending the small animals, doing some weeding in the garden, acting as cup-bearer at dinner, or, for the girls, doing simple weaving or helping in the kitchen. Carrying out these tasks gets them used to work early and trains them to understand their role in life.

On your country estate, the most important slave is the manager. Choose him carefully. If he is competent, then you will be free to devote your life to the dignified leisure that accords with your social station. If you select the wrong person, then productivity will fall, discipline will fail and you will find yourself constantly going back and forth from Rome, where your political and social responsibilities are based, to your estate to try to sort out the mess. I personally select and train my managers to ensure they are loyal agents for my interests.

I pick out two or three slaves in their early twenties who have impressed me with their attitude and promote them steadily. I rotate them thoroughly so that they gain experience of all the different aspects of the work that has to be done on the farm. If they let me down or fail to shine then I demote them as a punishment back to their previous position. I always praise those who do well and make sure that they are never seen to have benefited from flattering me. In fact if they try to tell me how wonderful I am I punish them so that they realise that this kind of nonsense is not to their advantage and that they would do better to work hard and deliver results.

The single most important piece of advice I can give you is not to appoint a manager from the kind of slaves who are good-looking and particularly not from the kind who waste their time hanging about in the city. The lazy slave who loves the taverns and brothels of urban life never stops dreaming about these things. Which is bad enough in your domestic slaves but when such a type is put in a position of authority over your estate this can cause speedy and irreparable damage to the fabric of your property.

You must choose a man who has been toughened up by farm work from his infancy, one who has been tested by experience. If you do not own a slave of this type, put in charge a slave who has worked steadily in the labour gangs. Make sure he is not a young man but in his thirties. If he is too young it will reduce his ability to order the other slaves to do things, especially the older slaves who will be reluctant to take their orders from a youth. But he shouldn't be too old either, as you don't want him to be unable to keep up with the heavy workload. He should have wide experience of the work on the farm or, if not, he must be something of a perfectionist so that you know he will learn what he needs to know properly. And he will need to know everything because in his position he cannot give orders to those who are teaching him how to do something. It probably doesn't matter much if he is illiterate so long as he has a good memory. In fact this can bring advantages in that if he cannot read or write then he will be far less able to falsify the accounts.

He should be skilled in animal husbandry, but he should also be in possession, as far as this is possible with a servile character, of a sense of empathy that means he can exercise authority without being either soft or cruel. He should always humour some of the better slaves, at the same time as being able to put up with the worse slaves, so that they will fear his sternness rather than detest his brutality. The best way for him to do this is by being thorough in his own job, which will make it far less likely that his subordinates will do the wrong thing because they will have been well directed. He will also act as an example for them to follow. There is no better way to supervise even the most wretched slaves than by making sure they work hard: make sure the overseer knows that you want him to watch them at all times. And get him to check on their work to see that everything has been done properly. Otherwise you may find that the foreman misses things and will give up on the difficult slaves, when in fact these are the very ones he should be watching most closely.

Incentivise your managers and overseers with bonuses to make them work harder and be more conscientious.

Allow them to keep their own money and possessions and let them cohabit with a woman of their choice, so long of course as the partnership is acceptable to you. Having a wife and children will calm them down and give them an even bigger stake in making your household prosper. You will win over your managers and foremen by treating them with a certain degree of respect. If they return the trust you have put in them by performing well, then it is also good to consult them about what needs to be done and by whom. If you do that, they will feel that you are treating them as almost an equal rather than looking down on them as a slave. They can also be motivated by being rewarded with more generous rations of food and clothing and the usual perks one uses to encourage slaves to work harder.

I teach my new managers the following things, which I think helps them to become more honest. (These are mostly well-known sayings and old-fashioned advice but they are all the more excellent for that.) I tell them not to use slaves to do anything except the master's business. Otherwise, you often find that new managers take advantage of their power by getting their slaves to run around doing errands for them, when the slaves should be working for the benefit of the estate. Managers should not eat unless it is with their underlings and they should eat the same food as them. Nothing is so likely to antagonise a weary slave as seeing his foreman tuck in to some tasty luxury when he himself is being fed plain fare. It also means that the manager will make sure the common bread is made properly, and that the meals are nutritious and wholesome.

I also teach new managers not to let anyone leave the estate unless I have personally authorised it. And if I am away, they should not authorise anyone unless there is a pressing need. I tell them not to carry out their own business on the side, as this will only distract them from doing your work. They must not invest your money in cattle or goods for trading purposes. Buying and selling purely for profit will just divert their attention from what really matters. What they must concentrate on is making sure your accounts are in good order. Otherwise you will end up owning a whole load of poor-quality goods that they have been unable to sell.

Make sure your manager does not let soothsayers and magicians on to the estate. These people always get the slaves overexcited and wound up by spreading their false stories and superstitions and selling them ridiculous spells and potions. The manager himself should go to town only when he has to buy things that are necessary for him to carry out his duties. A trip to the weekly market should be more than sufficient. You don't want a manager who likes to travel, but one who goes somewhere only when he will learn something by doing so. And even then only if the place is near enough that he can get back to the estate on the same day. Tell him not to allow new footpaths to be cut across the farm since it will only encourage outsiders to trespass on your land. Nor should he have guests round to stay unless it is one of your family or close friends.

Above all, teach your new manager that he should not think that he knows what he does not know, and that he must be passionate about learning what he is ignorant of.

Acquiring skills will make his work better. It will also cut out those needless mistakes that cause so much damage. Agriculture is not a difficult business. It requires your slaves to do the right thing repeatedly. If they learn this one guiding principle at the outset, they will not mess things up by causing harm through their ignorance. For one of the problems with farming is that it can take a long time and a lot of money to rectify mistakes.

Here is a checklist of the manager's duties to help you make sure he is doing what you need him to:

- Maintain strict discipline – but don't be needlessly cruel.
- Keep the slaves hard at work so they don't get involved in trouble.
- Observe the proper religious festivals (to keep the gods happy and the farm prosperous).
- Don't steal your master's possessions.
- Sort out arguments among the slaves: they are usually a quarrelsome bunch.
- Make sure the slaves get neither cold nor hungry.
- Remember: if you don't want slaves to make trouble, they're much less likely to.
- Reward good work and punish failure.
- Punish fairly those who have done wrong and in proportion to the damage caused by the crime.
- Stay on the estate.
- Be sober and don't go out to dinner.
- Don't think or act as if you're cleverer than your master.

- Don't treat your master's friends as if they were your own.

- Listen to everything your master tells you, and to whomever your master tells you to listen.

- Don't lend anyone money unless your master allows it.

- Insist on immediate repayment if your master does not permit a loan or its extension.

- Don't lend anyone seed, fodder, barley, wine or oil.

- Be on friendly terms with two or three neighbouring estates so you can borrow people, goods and implements when you need them.

- Go through the accounts with the master regularly.

- Don't use day labourers too much or for more than a day at a time.

- Don't buy anything without your master's approval.

- Don't keep anything secret from your master.

- Don't have any favourites among the slaves.

- Don't consult diviners, fortune-tellers or astrologers.

- Don't use seed corn sparingly – that way lies disaster.

- Make sure you understand how to do everything on the estate and if there are gaps in your knowledge fill them. You will then understand what the slaves themselves are thinking.

- Remember the slaves themselves will work more willingly for someone who understands their problems.

- Keep healthy and sleep well.
- Before going to bed make sure that the farm is secure, the animals are fed, and everyone is sleeping where they should be.
- Be first to get out of bed and last to go to bed.

The head of the female slaves is also an important position you should give great care to filling. Normally she will become the manager's wife. If she does her work well she will help to ensure that the estate produces a profitable income for you. Above all, she will make the farm as self-sufficient as possible by providing many domestic services, from weaving to mending to nursing the sick.

When the weather is bad and the women are unable to work outside, the manageress should occupy them with knitting and sewing. She should use some of the female slaves to do the job of spinning and weaving, with others having prepared it by carding. Making the slaves' clothes at home on the estate keeps your costs down.

When the weather is good, the manageress should always go around the estate and check that all the slaves have left the buildings and are not shirking in the barns. If she finds a malingerer she must interrogate him as to why he is not working. She must learn to tell whether it is the result of sickness or laziness, for slaves who are the latter will always claim the former. If she believes he is sick then she should take him to the sickbay. Even if she believes he is pretending to be ill, if she thinks he is doing this out of fatigue she can also use her discretion to let him have a day's rest in the sickbay. It is in the long run better to give a tired slave a rest rather than force him to work so hard that he really does become ill. It is, though, important to make sure that this discretion is not abused.

The manageress should never be sitting still. Her job is to rush about checking on everyone and making sure that the farm is operating smoothly and efficiently. She must go to the loom and teach the workers their new skills. Or she should learn a new skill from any slave who happens to know more than she does. She should check on the kitchens to see that the slaves' rations are being made properly. She must make sure that the kitchens, the cowsheds and, not least, the pigpens are properly cleaned. She should do the rounds of the sickbay, and even if there aren't any patients there she should have it cleaned so that it is fit to receive any slave that does fall sick.

If you do not pay great attention to the appointment of your manager and his wife you can quickly find yourself in a nightmare situation. I have heard some horror stories in my time: of a manager who sold part of the estate without his master's knowledge and then pretended to him that the extra money was in fact increased income from his efficient management of the estate. Or another who cut down most of the trees on the estate, sold them for 20,000 sesterces, added 10,000 to the accounts to boost the profit and pocketed the rest for himself. Bad managers will constantly sell off bits and pieces from your estate to boost the appearance of their performance. To begin with, you, the master, may be unaware of what is going on and may be delighted at how much more money you're getting from the estate. You will reward the manager with extra rations, fine clothes and time off. But later, when you realise that half of the farm has been sold off, all the things which the estate needs to generate its income, you will punish the manager very severely. But by then it will be too late and it will take you much time and money to put things right.

You must make sure you visit your estates regularly. Nothing is more likely to prevent your managers behaving in such a wanton fashion. For there can be no doubt that slaves are corrupted by their master's distance. And once corrupted, their greed and shamelessness only multiplies, until you might as well employ pirates to run your farms. In fact, if your estates are remote and it is difficult for you to visit except very occasionally, you would do well to consider having the land farmed by free tenants who will pay you a rent, rather than slaves, who, left to their own devices and safe in the knowledge that you are far away, will watch the estate gently crumble around them. They will let out the cattle for hire, feed the animals poorly, plough the land badly and pretend they have sown lots of seed when in fact they have sold off half of it for their own benefit. And when the meagre harvest does come in it will be further diminished by their constant theft and miscounting of the number of bushels that have been stored. You normally find that the manager and the general slaves are all in cahoots since they all stand to benefit from the arrangement. You, the master, will be the loser.

I often arrive unannounced to make sure I am seeing the estate as it really is and not as it has been brushed up for my visit. Then, once I have arrived, I summon the manager and ask for an immediate tour of inspection. I inspect every part of the estate and meet with slaves in all areas. I try to judge whether my absence has resulted in a relaxation of discipline and attention to detail. I look at the vines to see if they have been well tended, whether the trees look like they have had produce stolen from them. I have the animal stock counted along with the slaves and the farm equipment to see if it tallies with the manager's inventory. And if you do this year after year you can be assured that you will maintain a well-disciplined and ordered estate that will keep you in comfort into your old age. And however old you are, if you visit regularly you will make sure that the slaves do not take advantage of you and treat you with contempt rather than the respect you deserve.

In fact these visits can be something of an eye-opener about your own mortality. I recently visited an estate of mine and complained to the manager about a dilapidated old barn. The manager insisted it was not because he had been at fault but simply that the wood was old and the building falling down. I remember having this barn built when I was a young man! Then I complained to him about the gnarled old plane trees, and how poorly they were being kept. Again he replied that the problem was just that the trees were too old – but I remember planting them!

Visits can also reveal some nasty surprises. Once I visited an estate I used to own in southern Italy. On my tour of inspection, while walking through the fields of flowers, a woman who had been tied up with thick ropes and was holding a pitchfork threw herself at my feet. Her hair had been cut off, she was filthy and her tunic was ragged. 'Have pity on me, master,' she begged. 'I was born free but was captured by pirates and sold to your manager as a slave.' I believed her because she spoke elegantly and her facial features had a nobility that spoke of high birth, not servility.

She explained that my manager had tried to force her to share his bed. She begged me to free her and said that she would pay me back the 2,000 she had cost from her family back home across the seas from where the pirates had kidnapped her. She tore off her tunic and showed the terrible scars from where the manager had beaten her. I was very moved by this story.

'Do not worry, madam,' I said, 'you are free to return home and I do not need you to reimburse me. It is a disgrace for such high-born beauty and grace to be held in such conditions.' Instead, I summoned the manager, a shameless slave called Sosthenes, and said to him: 'You dreadful man – have you ever seen me treat even the most useless and worthless slaves in this way?' He then admitted that he had bought her from a pirate slave dealer because he fancied her. I demoted him on the spot from his position as manager, and had the woman bathed and dressed in fresh clothes and sent home.

Perhaps you think me mad to have done that, even though that woman was obviously freeborn. But it will benefit you to treat your slaves with a certain generosity of spirit. You should always be civil to them if they have worked well. Obviously you should not let them be insolent or give them free rein to speak their minds. But if they have positions of authority you should treat them respectfully. As I have said, I consult them, ask their opinions and even their advice if it is on a matter about which they know more than me. I find that slaves respond well to being treated in this way and go about their work with added enthusiasm. But I even apply this approach to those who have been punished by being chained up in the prison block. I visit them and check whether they are carefully chained, but also ask them if they feel they have been treated unjustly. For the lowliest slave is more likely to be punished unjustly for the simple reason that he has so many different layers of superior above him. And it is these simple, ignorant slaves who are most dangerous when they are smarting from being badly and cruelly treated. I even go so far as to let them make complaints about their overseers and, very occasionally, I uphold their complaints. This way the troublemakers are kept in check by being given a vent for their frustrations while the managers and overseers are kept honest by being aware of the fact that even the most useless slave can be asked to give feedback on their management.

For you will not be surprised to learn that slaves are often far more brutal towards each other than their master would ever be. In fact, you find that slaves are always jockeying for position, arguing over gradations of rank and quarrelling over all kinds of petty insults, actual or perceived. Those with the clearest tendency to bully their underlings must be themselves kept under control by fear of you if they are not to impose their own reign of terror on those beneath them. Otherwise you will find that your slaves become brutalised and worthless as a result. It is another reason why it is never a good idea to have too many slaves from the same ethnic origin working in the same household, because they seem to be particularly alert to minor differences and so are always quarrelling and fighting.

And in the final analysis, it is important to remember that your slaves are a significant investment for you and their value needs to be maintained. You must protect your property from any action that will reduce its value. Remember that it is illegal for someone to incite one of your slaves of previously good character to do something wrong. And it is illegal – and you can gain recompense – if someone praises your bad slaves for doing something wrong, such as running away or stealing; for one shouldn't make a bad slave even worse by praising him. Thus a man is to be found guilty of corrupting a slave whether he is making a good slave bad, or a bad slave worse. In fact there is a long list of acts for which you can gain financial compensation. No one is allowed to get your slaves to falsify their accounts, or have sex with them, or indulge in magic, or waste too much time at the games, or carry out treason, or cause your slave to live luxuriously by fiddling the books, or be disobedient, or gamble, or persuade him to submit to homosexual acts. For whether it derives from brutal treatment to other more subtle forms of corruption you must always be alert to factors that could erode the value of your assets.

·· COMMENTARY ··

Many upper-class Roman slave owners were influenced by ideas from Stoic philosophy, which insisted that a slave owner had possession only of the slave's body and not his soul, which remained free. This meant that they saw slaves as being intrinsically worth something as human beings and so should be treated with some respect. This extended to an obligation to treat them decently and fairly in the same way that hired labourers should be. It is impossible to know the extent to which such ideas penetrated society more widely. It would be nice to think that most Roman masters believed that they had an obligation to all their dependants, including their slaves, even if this was motivated by self-interest and the desire to preserve their assets.

The training of slaves was influenced heavily by the tasks which they were intended to perform. Field workers needed little and could be put straight to work. The surviving Roman agricultural manuals make it clear that it was important to select ambitious slaves to serve as overseers, since it was these individuals who would keep the estate running smoothly on a day-to-day basis. Within larger urban households domestic slaves would probably be trained up by other more senior slaves, rather than by the master himself. It is impossible to tell how many slaves had to be 'broken'. One of the reasons that some Romans favoured home-bred slaves was that they had grown up accustomed to slavery. The fact that Seneca urges owners to show pity towards new slaves when they are forced to carry out degrading tasks suggests that most masters did not. Seneca is probably best seen as arguing against common practice, as otherwise his text would have had little interest to his Roman readership.

Slave rations are listed in the agricultural manuals and are unsurprisingly plain. Clothing is similarly rough and basic. Slaves may have been able to supplement their rations by means of foraging, keeping their own animals and maintaining their own kitchen gardens. Those who worked in chain gangs probably had little opportunity to do any of these things. Slaves in a more senior position were probably allowed greater indulgence to soften their existence.

One of the reasons why many Roman texts are ambivalent about the economic benefits of using slaves to farm estates was that they required so much supervision to keep them working. It was assumed that slaves would be trying hard to work as little as possible, whereas the free tenant had a vested interest in making the land productive. The use of slaves also contrasted with the Roman ideal of the honest yeoman, on whom the success of the republic had been built. It seemed wrong that the land was now being farmed by imported slave labour and could hardly, therefore, be seen as progress. Often the purpose of owning huge estates seems to have been little more than ostentatious display, and the use of a large servile workforce was part of this ostentation. Most owners of large estates probably had their land farmed by a variety of slave and free labour.

The treatment of old and sick slaves also probably varied considerably. The emperor Claudius issued an edict in an attempt to stop people from dumping them on the Tiber island. This may have represented simply a vain attempt to prevent a social nuisance impacting on the centre of Rome rather than any attempt to improve the slaves' lot. Seneca advocated greater leniency and decency in the treatment of slaves than most Romans but even Seneca, the source for the story of the old door-keeper, had no recollection of his old childhood play-mate. It is hard to see that most Romans would have spent much money on an old asset once it had stopped giving a reasonable return in the form of continued service unless there was some personal reason for doing so, such as supporting an old nursemaid.

At the other end of the age spectrum, child slaves are assumed in one legal text to be working by the age of five. This is not surprising since there was no need for them to be educated and they would have been able to carry out some small tasks around the farm or household.

The farm manager was clearly the most important individual for the owner of an estate. The bad manager is a recurrent theme of ancient literature, including the Bible. Given that most large landowners were absentee for at least part of the year, they were entirely reliant on this individual to keep their asset producing the surplus that would help pay for their life of dignified leisure in the city. This is why so much emphasis was placed on the importance of visiting estates. Absence, it was assumed, bred contempt, which would lead to the land and farm buildings not being maintained properly and yields declining rapidly as a result.

Slaves were expensive and each owner had to balance

the treatment of his slaves with the need to keep them working and, to some extent, incentivised. Brutal treatment doubtless occurred occasionally but it could not be the norm, since this would soon wear out the servile assets. In the country, dividing the slaves into a 'them and us', whereby a small group of overseers were motivated by material rewards and the ultimate goal of freedom, probably worked well to keep the system functioning efficiently.

On ancient farming, see Cato *On Agriculture*. On the goal of self-sufficiency, see Varro *On Agriculture* 1.16. For ancient discussion of whether it was better to have your land farmed by slaves or free tenants, see Columella *On Agriculture* 1.7. On gang labour see Pliny the Elder *Natural History* 18.4. The story of a falling-down barn as a reminder of old age is recounted in Seneca *Letters* 12, as is the story of the former playmate. On herdsmen, see Varro *On Agriculture* 2.10. Managers are described in Varro *On Agriculture* 1.17 and Columella *On Agriculture* 1.8. Cato *On Agriculture* 5 lists the duties of the manager. For the manager's wife, see Columella *On Agriculture* 12.3. The problems created by a bad manager are described in Cicero *Against Verres* 2.3.50. The story of the woman who had been captured by pirates and is found being abused on an inspection can be read in the novel *Leucippe and Clitophon* by Achilles Tatius 5.17. Cato's attitudes to slaves can be seen in Plutarch's *Life of Cato the Elder* 4.4, 5.2 and 21.1.

· CHAPTER III ·

SEX AND SLAVES

I HAD A CURIOUS DREAM the other night. I dreamt that I entered the small storeroom in which a number of my slaves sleep, selected a young female of German descent, and then proceeded to have intercourse with her. I was troubled that this might be interpreted as signalling that I would become a slave, since I was seen to be consorting with them, or worse that my descendants would end up in the servile class. Perturbed by such thoughts, I consulted a dream-interpreter, called Artemidorus, who lives in the town.

'Do not be anxious,' he assured me, 'for dreaming of sex with your slave is auspicious because it shows that the dreamer will derive pleasure from his possessions.'

Of course! Now he had explained it to me, the meaning was clear. I have always tried to be abstemious when it comes to taking advantage of my high social position for the purposes of pleasure, but the gods were telling me to relax and enjoy myself. It is, incidentally, strange how often slaves feature in dreams, even in the dreams of slaves. Artemidorus told me that he knew of a slave who dreamt that his penis was stroked and aroused by his master's hand, and had consulted him in the hope that this would indicate that he would please his master in some way. Sadly for the slave in this case it did not signify any benefit. Instead it meant that he would be bound to a pillar and receive many strokes from a whip.

The great philosopher emperor, Marcus Aurelius, was proud of the fact that he owned two beautiful slaves but had not taken advantage of them. But we would certainly be too stern if we expected most masters to behave with such self-control. It is perfectly normal for an owner to derive sexual pleasure from his young slaves. I have a youth who is my current favourite. He is fourteen and is both keen and happy to do what his master wants. After all, where is the shame in carrying out your master's wishes? It's perfectly normal! As I have mentioned, if you wish to purchase yourself a boy as a pet, you would be well advised to go the Saepta Julia and ask to see if they have any Egyptians in the back. These are well suited for such a task, having fair skin, shiny eyes, a low brow, a narrow nose, long unbraided hair and red lips. As for young female slaves, you might consider a blonde-haired Batavian. Whatever your desire, just be careful about getting carried away when haggling over the price and thinking with your passion and not your head. That is when middle-aged men, who are old enough to know far better, end up acting, and paying, like fools.

I like to reward my favourites with small gifts to show them that they are special to me. The slave girls are always pleased to receive some clothes that my wife has finished with. My wife is, of course, completely relaxed about these dalliances. What man is without peccadilloes of this kind? Naturally, however, it would be unthinkable for her to indulge in any such acts with her male slaves. For that would bring great shame on the household and my name.

It is an occupational hazard that you will get some of your slave girls pregnant. They often seem delighted to have acquired some closer link with their master. I like to treat these offspring with greater indulgence than I would normal slaves, and give them slightly better rations and easier work. I mentioned that I like to use them to look after my real children, because they do, after all, share some of my blood and so can be relied upon to be more loyal and diligent. Obviously I cannot be expected to treat all my illegitimate offspring in such a way. So if when born they look sickly, or if I already have a sufficient number of them in the household, I order the mothers to expose the infants by leaving them at the dump. Which reminds me, I heard a very amusing joke about this the other day. One day an idiot had a child by a slave girl, and his father advised him to kill it. But he replied, 'First, you kill your own children, then you can talk about me killing mine.'

It is important, though, that you do not allow your female slaves to be exploited for immoral sexual purposes. So whenever I sell a female slave who is still in possession of her looks, I stipulate in the contract of sale that her new owner will not prostitute her. Indeed, the divine emperor Vespasian promulgated a decree which upheld conditions of that sort, whereby if any woman had been sold on condition that she should not be employed as a prostitute, and she had been so prostituted, then she should become free. He also ordered that if the buyer were later to sell her to someone else without imposing the same condition, she should become free in accordance with the conditions of the original sale, and become the freedwoman of the person who had originally sold her.

Of course, slaves themselves also wish to have sex with each other and many wish to enter into family relationships. It is completely within your power as to whether you allow them such unions. Slaves cannot legally marry but they can be allowed to enter into an informal bond between themselves. Generally, when I am approached by two of my household slaves I agree to such a union as it generates goodwill, whereas a refusal will only result in spite. Marriage-type relations within the household also promote stability. I recommend that you allow them to raise a family. This brings with it a number of advantages. It makes them contented and more likely to work harder to earn their freedom; it provides 'hostages', so to speak, making it less likely that their parents will ever try to run away; and, above all, it means that there will be another generation of home-bred slaves to replace them once the parents have been freed or died, slaves who will be a genuine part of the family and not just outsiders bought for money.

Occasionally, however, I do have to refuse to allow the formation of a lasting relationship. This is usually because I consider the union to be between slaves with negative characteristics or between malcontents who would only use the relationship as an opportunity to foment even greater unrest. In this case, I sell one of the pair to prevent anything going on behind my back. Thankfully, this is rare and perhaps a third of all my slaves are married in the non-legal sense, although if they ever become free their marriages will be recognised in law.

More casual sexual relations are difficult to regulate. There are usually insufficient women to go round in my country estates and so they need to be shared out. I divide off the slave women's quarters from the men's quarters by means of a bolted door, so that nothing untoward can go on. This ensures that the slaves do not have children without my approval. Frequent sexual activity weakens the males for their daily work, which in the farm is vigorous and physical. So what I do is occasionally allow the male slaves access to the women's quarters, not so rarely as to cause discontent and not so frequently as to cause a decline in productivity.

Generally I prefer to manage my slaves' relationships and assign a longer-term partner to them. This enables me to select pairings that will, in my opinion, work well both practically and in the issue of child-rearing. It is an advantage for all to have children. I grant any slave woman of mine who has given birth to three live sons exemption from work. To a woman who has produced more than three male heirs I give her her freedom. Strangely, the moral of the Aesop fable of the dove and the crow states that 'the most pitiful slaves are those who beget children in servitude'. I presume this is because they fear that their children will be sold off and the family broken up as a result. This is something I rarely do except in cases of ill discipline.

Breeding slaves is a useful and profitable exercise but you should bear in mind that it does involve capital outlay and is time-consuming. It is simple enough when dealing with farm slaves. Since they stay on the farm all day all that is required is for a female to be assigned to them. It is more complicated when it comes to shepherds who tend the flocks in the mountain valleys and woodlands. They shelter in makeshift huts and lead a rugged existence. It is therefore advisable to send women along with them for company and to prepare them food, but make sure that they are strong and capable of surviving in such a harsh environment. They often seem to do just as good a job as the menfolk, tending to the herd, fetching firewood, or managing their huts. When it comes to feeding their offspring, I merely remark that they suckle them while they work, carrying logs and babies at the breast at the same time. It just goes to show how soft and contemptible new mothers are today, who lie about for days under mosquito nets to recuperate.

The head-slave – or bailiff or overseer, as you might also call them – should be treated with more generosity when it comes to women as a reward and incentive for their loyalty. He should be given a woman companion not only to keep him company but, as we have seen, as a help to him in the execution of his important tasks. The overseer should be warned not to become intimate with a member of the household without your say-so, and much less with an outsider, since you will want to ensure that his partner is capable of performing this important role. I like to invite my bailiffs to dine with me to discuss possible partners, as a way of making them feel included in such an important decision for all of us.

When selecting such a woman, who will in effect be the farm's manageress, you should consider the woman who has shown the greatest moderation when it comes to food, wine, sleep and sex. Also, choose one who seems to have the best memory, who is the most careful in the performance of her tasks, and is most eager to please her master. This is something you can encourage by showing her how happy you are when she has pleased you and likewise how disappointed when she has fallen short. In short, you must train her to want the household to prosper and to feel that she shares in its success. Encourage her to develop a sense of justice by giving greater benefits to slaves who deserve them and not to those who do not. Make it clear to her that good and honest service will bring greater wealth and freedom than will laziness and thieving. She will then become just the kind of woman you can trust in this important position.

Urban slaves are easier to deal with because it is easier to monitor their relationships under your own roof. Spotting a coupling that might prove beneficial and fruitful can almost become something of a parlour game for you and your wife. If you, as the head of the household, behave justly and carefully in this way, you will find that your number of slaves can increase significantly. But you would do well not to rely solely on home-breeding to meet all of your slave requirements. Illness, injury and premature death will always mean that your body of slaves is being whittled away. It is also useful to bring in some outside blood from time to time to freshen up the stock, as it were, and shake up the slaves you already own and who may have grown too comfortable in their existence. I like to maintain a mix of about half home-breds and half bought in from outside. Yet, for all that, it must be accepted that home-bred slaves are a joy and reflect well on the status of the family. They increase the value of our estates and provide loyal and deferential service. They are living proof of a household that is cohesive and multiplying, in the same way that a well-run state should be.

·· COMMENTARY ··

Slaves feature repeatedly in the *Interpretation of Dreams* by Artemidorus, which dates from the second century AD, and sometimes in a sexual way. This might suggest that the Roman subconscious was deeply affected by the hierarchical and repressive world around it. But the Romans did not interpret dreams in such a Freudian, internalised or sexualised way. They preferred to see dreams as providing a divinely inspired message concerning the dreamer's future. In a world where slavery marked the bottom layer of society, prophecies about the future contained references to slavery as part of their dramatic effect. It is interesting that mention is made of slaves having their dreams interpreted. This suggests that some slaves had sufficient money to consult dream-interpreters, and that they thought it was worth spending on such things. It goes to show that slaves were worried about the future just as free people were. Slaves may have lived in servitude but that did not mean that they were devoid of hope or interest in what might happen to them.

There is plenty of evidence for the sexual abuse of slaves. A combination of the powerful position that the master had over his slaves and their lack of basic rights means that this should not come as a surprise. The fact that the philosopher emperor Marcus Aurelius was proud of himself for resisting the temptations posed by two beautiful slaves suggests that this is not a course that most masters would have taken. There was little stigma attached in masters having sex with boys and adolescent males: all slaves were there for the master to take advantage of if he so wished, whatever their sex or age. Many masters would have been classified as paedophiles in the modern world. Unwanted slave pregnancies were sufficiently common to joke about (see the *Laughter Lover*, attributed to Hierocles and Philagrius, for various examples). There is a hint of the resentment sexual abuse could cause in Petronius's *Satyricon* (ch. 57), when a freedman notes that, 'I bought freedom for the slave woman who had shared my bed, so that no one could wipe his filthy hands on her breast.' In the same work (ch. 75), Trimalchio says he had as a boy become his master's favourite for fourteen years, but defends it by saying, 'I mean, what's wrong with doing what your master wants?' That is probably how most masters justified their behaviour, or at least they would have if they had felt the need to.

As they saw it, their slaves were their possessions to be used as they saw fit.

We do not know what slaves themselves thought about such treatment. It is reasonable to assume that sexual abuse will have had a significant negative psychological impact. Modern studies find that victims of such abuse are left demoralised, deferential and unassertive. In ancient dream interpretation (Artemidorus 3.28), it is perhaps not surprising that a mouse signifies a household slave as it lives in the house and is 'timid'. Suicide attempts were sufficiently common to merit legal opinion, which stated that sellers were obliged to reveal to prospective buyers if the slave had tried to kill him or herself (*Digest* 21.1.23.3; 21.1.1.1). Suicide, or attempted suicide, is not in itself a sign of mental illness, but it does point to profound stresses within an individual's life.

Or perhaps Roman slaves did not experience abuse as abuse. Perhaps they did rationalise it in the way that Trimalchio did. And, if it could be shown that they had no real sense of self, we might assume that they would not have been strongly affected by this kind of treatment. Only someone with a sense of his or her own value can be humiliated and degraded. But the evidence suggests that many slaves had strong views about justice and their own worth. Artemidorus describes how many slaves 'long for freedom' and made great sacrifices to acquire it (Artemidorus 2.3). The Delphic manumission inscriptions show that many slaves paid large sums to secure their freedom, often at an uncertain future date, typically on their master's death. Freedmen tombs often make strong statements of personal achievement and self-worth.

The evidence is that many, perhaps most, slaves resented or even hated their social position and so faced intensely powerful stresses in their lives, some of it in the form of sexual abuse. Modern mental health research, and perhaps even common sense, tells us that such conditions will have had a detrimental impact on their psychological well-being and resulted in a generally poor level of mental health in the overall servile population. In that case, slaves probably had a high incidence of mental disorders, even if the form that those disorders took might have been very different to those of the modern world.

CHAPTER IV

WHAT MAKES A GOOD SLAVE?

I AM A PRACTICAL MAN AND this is a practical book. I have little time for the fancy philosophies of the Greeks and even less for those who like to tie themselves up with the sophistries of logic. But I do think that it will help you manage your slaves better if you properly understand how best to think about them. To know what makes a slave a slave is to know what makes a master a master. So I hope you will bear with me while I explain to you what might be termed the philosophy of slavery.

We Romans all know that free is to slave as good is to bad. But there have been Greeks who questioned whether the fact that slaves are social inferiors means that they are necessarily also moral inferiors. And if slaves are not less moral than their masters they wondered whether slavery itself could ever be justified. The philosopher Aristotle, as I mentioned earlier, was of the view that it was natural for slaves to be slaves, since barbarians were inherently inferior to Greeks and so were naturally suited to be the slaves of the superior Greeks.

I'm not sure if anyone ever actually believed this, but it is certainly true to say that the Greeks did see slavery in black-and-white terms. So if a free man became a slave he remained, at heart, naturally free, whereas any barbarian who was enslaved merely got his just deserts.

I once heard two Greeks arguing vociferously about something (I don't recall what it was). As it happened one of the men was a slave and, in the end, the free man, who seemed to be losing the argument to his clever opponent, threw up his arms in despair and said, 'What would you know anyway? You're just a slave!' At which the slave responded by smiling sweetly and saying: 'But can you really tell the difference between a free man and a slave?' The free citizen insisted that he knew that he was free but that the slave was not. But this merely goaded the slave into arguing more, in the same way that fighting-cocks get increasingly aggressive when they are struck. So he asked the citizen what the basis was of his knowledge about their status in society. How did he know for certain that his mother hadn't secretly been having sex with her slaves and that one of them was his father? He claimed that there were many famous Athenians who were later revealed to have been smuggled in as infants and raised by Athenian parents when in fact they were outsiders – how did he know for sure he was not one of them?

As you can see, he was one of those too-clever-by-half slaves. In the end his opponent simply said that whatever smart arguments the slave made about not being able to be 100 per cent certain that a slave is actually a slave, or a citizen is really a free man, one thing was for sure and that was that the slave was being held in a condition of slavery. But the slave was having none of it.

'Oh, come on!' he said, 'Do you think that everyone who is being held in slavery is a real slave? There are plenty of free men who are being held unjustly as slaves. You often see them appealing in the law courts and producing evidence to prove that they are free. Tens of thousands of people have suffered this misfortune. And when a free Athenian is taken prisoner in war and is shipped off to Persia or Sicily and sold there, we don't say that he is now a slave. We say he is still, in truth, free. But if a Persian or Sicilian is brought here we certainly don't say that he is still free.'

So the citizen said that it was the way in which he was treated that made him a slave. But the slave was too clever for that.

'So what,' he said, 'if I am fed by my master, do what he says, and get punished if I don't – that would make his sons his slaves too. They have to do whatever their father tells them and are beaten if they don't.'

He added that it would also make schoolboys the slaves of their teachers. The free man countered that teachers and fathers don't chain up their sons and pupils, or sell them or send them to work in the treadmill. Only masters do that to slaves. But the slave replied that there are many places where fathers do behave like that towards their sons. He himself knew several people who had sold children into slavery because they needed the money. But that did not make their remaining sons slaves.

The point the slave was making was that no matter how obvious it might seem that slaves are naturally servile and worthless, it is possible for them to become free and for their children to be as free as anyone. And in the same way, if a free man suffers the misfortune of being captured and sold off as a slave then he is to all intents and purposes a slave and cannot be distinguished from any other slave. There is nothing natural about slavery.

Thankfully, the people who were listening to this argument were getting bored by the slave's refusal to accept any evidence, and by his clever arguments. So they asked him what a slave actually is. Someone said that if a person has full rights of ownership over another, meaning that he is able to do whatever he wants with him, just as he could with any other piece of his property, then that person is correctly described as being the slave of the man who owns him. But the slave asked what 'full rights of ownership' meant. After all, there were many people who appeared to own a house or a horse or something when it actually transpired that they had no legal right to them. In the same way, a man or woman might be owned unjustly. The first slaves must have been captured in war because they could not have been born to slaves. In other words, they had been free, and were then forced into servitude, which hardly seems very moral and is hard to defend at all. It certainly isn't possible to say that such people were naturally slaves to start with because they weren't – they were free. And if they had managed to run away they would have been free again so would have returned to their former status.

Someone who was watching the argument suggested that although these people were clearly not slaves, their children and grandchildren were because they were born

slaves. 'But how?' replied the slave. 'If it is being captured that makes a man a slave, then shouldn't the term
be applied to those who are captured themselves much
more than to the descendants? If it is not that but birth
which is the criterion, then it is clear that since those
who were captured were free men, their children could
not be slaves either.'

Perhaps, the slave went on, the word 'slave' originally
just meant someone with a servile character. For we all
know free men who have the traits of slaves and slaves
who have a noble disposition. It's like the terms 'noble'
and 'well born': people first used them to refer to those
who were well born in terms of virtue and their behaviour, not in reference to who their parents were. Slaves are
not naturally bad or worthless any more than free men
are naturally good. People have simply stopped thinking
about what they are saying and use the terms wrongly.
In fact it is those who behave in a morally worthless way
who are the true slaves, whether they are actually slaves
or have been born free.

The Greeks could have argued all night. What *we* have
to realise is that while free is to slave as good is to bad,
that does not necessarily imply that all slaves are bad –
they can only be so regarded when they behave slavishly.
The moral status of a person is a reflection of the quality
of their soul. Their social status is irrelevant to this question. For it is vital that *we* understand this one fact: that
slaves are human beings and should be treated as such.

Those masters who have both wisdom and learning
realise that they must live on close terms with their slaves.
They are, after all, the people with whom you share your

roof. The vagaries of chance are so great that you should remember that it could easily have been you who ended up enslaved instead of being the master. That is why it is ridiculous when people say they would be ashamed to have dinner with a slave. Why? What reason is there to be so arrogant other than the dreadful practice of most masters nowadays, that they must be surrounded by a whole crowd of slaves. The master today stuffs his face until his stomach is so bloated and distended that it can barely digest the vast quantities of rich delicacies which have been crammed into it. Then in a great effort of straining he vomits it all back out again.

While he does this, his wretched slaves aren't allowed to so much as utter a sound but have to stand silently or else get thrashed. Not even an unintentional hiccough is permitted in case it distracts the master from his huge feat of gormandising. Any noise from the slaves will bring the most severe punishment. All evening, while the master repeatedly fills and empties his stomach, they stand there, silently shivering in hunger and fear lest their grumbling stomachs disturb their master from his table.

When masters treat their slaves like this, is it any surprise that they go round gossiping about him behind his back? By contrast, those slaves who were allowed to speak not just in front of their master but actually with him, were prepared to die for him so great was their loyalty. They would willingly stand between him and any danger that threatened him. They might talk when they served him his dinner, but they kept silent when they were being tortured by his enemies for information that might harm him.

If you think slaves are our enemies then you should remember that they are enemies only because we make them so. There are so many ways in which people treat them cruelly and inhumanely, as if they were no more than dumb animals rather than human beings. When, for example, we recline on our couches to dine, while they have to stand around and wait to clear up the vomit from those who have either eaten or drunk too much, or more likely both. Or when some poor slave has the job of carving expensive pheasants and fowl. He skilfully guides his well-trained hand around the bird's breast and rump as he carves it up. But he won't get any of the meat, poor man. He lives for no other purpose than to skilfully carve up roast chicken. The master who feels he has to teach a slave this skill is more to be pitied than the slave who has no choice but to learn it.

Another slave pours the wine. The young man is dressed like a woman and struggles to look as youthful as he can, although signs of his manhood are starting to appear. Another slave's job is to measure how the guests behave. He stands there nervously and makes a note of those who behave so outrageously that they are worth inviting back tomorrow. There are slaves who prepare the menu and know every detail of their master's taste. They know exactly what will perk up his taste buds and *amuse* his *bouche*, as it were. They know what kinds of presentation please him, what kind of novel cuisine will liven him up when he feels sick. They understand what bores him and when he will crave certain things. Needless to say, the master wouldn't dream of eating with these cooks because he thinks it would be beneath him to share a table with a slave.

I once saw the master of a certain slave leave him standing outside in the rain while his guests were invited inside to dine. The master later put him up for sale among a group of particularly worthless slaves – the kind who were sold in the first lot of the day when the auctioneer is just warming up. And what became of this supposedly worthless slave? Why, he became a notoriously powerful freedman, who rose to a position of great influence under the emperor. He ended up with thirty large onyx columns in his dining room. And he made sure he paid his old master back for the contempt with which he had treated him.

You must think carefully about the fact that the man whom you call your slave was born in the same way as you, breathes like you, and dies like you. You must see through his servile exterior and recognise the free man within, in the same way that he can see your inner slave. Fate is always bringing men down and making even those of the highest birth grovel in the dirt. Do you really think you should disrespect a slave whose status is one to which you yourself might one day be reduced, if chance wishes it so?

I don't want to give you a lecture about how to treat your slaves. What I really want to say to you is this. Treat your slaves as you would wish to be treated by your own superior. Whenever you think about how much power you have over your slaves, remember how much power your master has over you. And if you object that you don't have a master then remember what chance can do and how there may well come a day when you do have one.

So forgive your slaves when they make mistakes, have conversations with them, be courteous to them, share a meal with them. At this point all those who go in for luxurious living will scream at me: what a disgusting and undignified way to behave! But can't you see that this was how our great ancestors wanted us to behave towards our slaves? They called them 'members of the household' and the master 'head of the household' because they were all part of the same family unit. They gave masters a position of respect and the power to administer justice within the household. They thought the household was a miniature version of the state.

So, you will ask, you want me to invite all my slaves to dinner every night, do you? Not more than you invite your children, I say. You shouldn't just ignore people who work for you because they carry out low-status jobs. You can't judge a mule-herder just because he has a miserable job. It's his moral character that really counts. Jobs are assigned by chance, but everyone has their own moral character, which is something they themselves can develop. You must invite some people to have dinner with you because they deserve it, and others so that they are encouraged to deserve it in the future. If there is something slavish in your slaves' characters, then mixing in the company of free men such as yourself will drive it out of them.

You see, you shouldn't draw your friends only from among those of a similar class. If you look carefully, you'll find friends in your own home too. Good wood often warps if no craftsman uses it. But if you try it you will find that you have lots of good wood to use. Just like when you are buying a horse, you don't examine just the saddle, you look at the horse underneath. So you are a fool if you judge a man by his clothes or social status. The man who you see as a slave might well be free in his heart.

In fact, we are all slaves in our hearts. Some are slaves to sex, others to money, some to fame, others to status. All of us are slaves to hope and fear. Let me give you some examples of slavish behaviour among the so-called nobility. I know a man of consular rank who acts like the slave of an old woman because he is desperate to inherit her fortune. Then there is the wealthy old man who lusts after some young slave girl and thinks he can win over her affections by charm rather than force. I can think of many sons of the best families who have become infatuated with actors and actresses on the stage; and there is no kind of slavery more dishonourable than that which is entered into voluntarily. So you shouldn't let these kinds of people stop you from fraternising with your slaves and treating them pleasantly and not as their arrogant superior. Let your slaves respect rather than fear you.

I dare say that some people will accuse me of inciting slaves to revolt and overthrow their masters. They will say that slaves, as befits those of low status, must treat us, their masters, with respect and deference. But these people want to be treated better than a god. If you are respected you are also loved, and love cannot be mixed up with fear. So you must realise that you don't want your slaves to fear you, and that when you punish them you should try to do so with words. Beatings should really be reserved for punishing beasts. We have so much luxury that we get mad at every little thing that doesn't please us completely. We are acting like tyrants, for they have fits of anger that are completely inappropriate for their position of power. But that power means that no one will remonstrate with them. And in reality the things that displease us are so minor that they cannot harm us. So what if we don't get exactly the right delicacy served up in exactly the right way? By throwing great tantrums we actually just do ourselves more harm. Anyway, I don't want to preach to you. Managing slaves is difficult and often annoying but you should try to keep these ideals in the back of your mind even if in reality you fall short of them. Otherwise you will find that you soon slip into bad habits and you will start treating your slaves as if you are a despot and they are dumb animals.

You must remember that if slaves are not naturally slavish then you are not naturally masterful. Status is not enough: you have to prove it by your actions. Your slaves also, of course, have to show that they are not slavish, by behaving nobly and as a free man would be expected to. If slaves continually sink into bad behaviour then they cannot be surprised if people think they have a natural disposition to vice, as well as an inbuilt moral inferiority which makes them incapable of aspiring to any of the higher things in life.

I want to prove to you that slaves are capable of behaving in the best possible manner. They are not all cheeky or cunning, but can be both loyal and noble. Instead, because their souls remain free, they are able to behave with the utmost virtue. There are many people who question whether a slave is able to do his master a good turn. In fact, slaves often go well beyond what is required of them in order to help their masters. There are many examples of slaves who have fought to protect their masters without any regard for their own safety, and even when pierced through with multiple wounds have kept on fighting until the last drop of blood has left their veins, and by doing so have bought their masters enough time to escape. Then there are those slaves who have refused to betray their master's secrets even when threatened and tortured to the point of death.

In many ways, examples of slaves behaving in a most virtuous way like this are all the more remarkable for their rarity. Such acts are to be praised even more than comparable ones by free men, because they have been done by those who have to labour under the constraints of necessity. But despite the unpleasant authority that their masters have over them, the love of these slaves for their masters has overcome any resentment they may feel at serving as a slave.

And in fact these noble slaves are not so rare. When the town of Grumentum was being besieged and had become completely desperate, two runaway slaves crossed over and gave assistance to the enemy. Later, when the victorious army was running amok throughout the captured city, these two ran on ahead by a route that was well known to them to the house in which they had served as slaves, and they helped their mistress escape. When any of the invaders asked who she was, the slaves said she was their mistress and they were taking her away to execute her because she had treated them so cruelly. But in fact they brought her outside the city walls and hid her very carefully until the enemy's soldiers had had their fill of slaughter and pillaging. Then they set their mistress free again. She in return freed them both immediately; she certainly didn't feel degraded by having her life saved by people over whom she had the power of life and death. Indeed, she became famous and her generosity became an example for all Romans.

Or there is the story of a high-ranking official called Paulus, who was lying on his couch having dinner, wearing a ring on which was inlaid a large gem engraved with a portrait of the emperor Tiberius. He stood up and relieved himself in the chamber pot. A notorious informer called Maro noticed this, and saw a golden opportunity to have Paulus indicted for polluting the emperor's image, thereby gaining himself a large reward. But Paulus's slave also saw what his master had done. Immediately the slave took the ring from his drunken master's finger and put it on his own. So when Maro appealed to the other diners as witnesses that the emperor's image had been violated, the slave simply showed them that the ring was on his own hand.

When the divine Augustus was emperor, dinner parties had not yet become so dangerous but they could cause problems. A senator called Rufus was so drunk that he claimed out loud during a dinner that the emperor would not return safely from a journey he was about to undertake, because all the bulls that were going to be sacrificed to ensure his safe return would actually be hoping for the opposite. The following morning, the slave who had been standing at the bottom of Rufus's couch during the dinner told him what he had said during the meal while he was drunk. The slave urged him to go and confess it to Augustus before someone else informed the emperor. Rufus agreed and went to see Augustus. He swore that he hadn't realised what he was saying the previous evening and prayed that any misfortune would land on his own head and not the emperor's. He begged Caesar to forgive him. When the emperor said that he would do so, Rufus replied that no one would believe it unless the emperor gave him a present. He then asked for a very generous amount of money. And Augustus gave it to him, saying that he wouldn't ever be able to afford to get really angry with Rufus. Of course, the emperor acted extremely generously here in forgiving the foolish Rufus, but it was the slave who really saved his master. It goes without saying that he was freed at once by Rufus.

I could go on and on listing the many good qualities that have been found to lie in the heart of a slave. There was the case of Urbinus. He had been sentenced to death and was hiding on his estate at Reate. When his hiding place was betrayed, one of his slaves put on his ring and clothes and, pretending to be his master, lay down in his master's bedroom. The soldiers sent to get Urbinus broke in to the house, found the slave, who calmly offered them his neck. He received the executioner's blow as resolutely as Urbinus ever could have. After Urbinus had been pardoned, he had a tomb made for his slave with an inscription describing his great act of virtue.

Or take the case of the goodwill a slave showed his master despite having himself been recently punished by him. The master, Antius Restio, was outlawed and fled into the night on his own. His slaves started to plunder his property, all except one who had been chained up and branded on the forehead. The other slaves released him but, instead of joining in the pillaging, he followed after his fugitive master. He found him and Restio naturally feared that he was out to avenge his cruel punishment. But the slave assured him that he understood that his degrading punishment had been the fault of fortune not his master. He then hid Restio and fetched him supplies. Soon after, when he realised that soldiers were approaching, he strangled an old man who happened to be nearby, built a funeral pyre and threw the corpse on to it. He set it on fire and told anyone who came by that it was Restio who had died, which he deserved to have done for having branded him. Everyone believed the story, the soldiers went away, and Restio was saved.

Similarly, when Caepio's plot to murder Augustus had been uncovered and he had been condemned to death, one of his slaves carried him down to the Tiber in a chest and managed to take him to his estate in the country during the night. Later he took him on board a boat, was shipwrecked with him, and hid his master in Naples. Even when the pair was arrested, the slave refused to give any information that might incriminate his master. Or there was the time when the city of Padua was being pressured by Asinius Pollio to supply him with arms and money and many owners went into hiding as a result. Pollio offered rewards and freedom to any slaves who betrayed their masters, but not a single one did so.

Mark Antony was once accused of a sexual offence and the prosecutors demanded that a certain slave of his, I can't remember his name, be tortured for evidence since he had been carrying the lantern when the crime was committed. The interrogation could only happen if his master agreed and Mark Anthony was unwilling, perhaps fearing what the slave might say under duress. But despite realising that it would mean his own torture, the slave urged his master to hand him over, promising that he would not say anything incriminating. Despite being severely tortured, he revealed nothing.

Some slaves have even preferred death to being separated from their masters. For example, when Gaius Vettius was arrested by his own troops so they could hand him over to Pompey, his slave killed him and then committed suicide so as not to survive his master. What nobility of character! And when Gaius Gracchus was killed, his loyal slave Euporus, who had been an inseparable companion, killed himself over Gracchus's dead body by ripping open his stomach with his own hand.

It is not only male slaves who can display these fine characteristics. There is one particularly memorable action performed by slave women, and you'll find it difficult to find a better example of a deed benefiting the state that was performed by any noblewoman.

It is well known that 7 July is the festival of slave women. On that day free women and their slaves sacrifice to Juno Caprotina beneath a wild fig tree. This commemorates the great courage shown by slave women in defence of the honour of Rome. For after Rome had been sacked in 390 BC, the state was in dire straits. The neighbouring tribes, looking for an opportunity to invade Roman territory, appointed Postumius Livius, the dictator of Fidenae, to command them. He demanded that the Roman senate hand over all mothers and unmarried girls if they wanted to keep what was left of their state. The senate hesitated about what to do. But a slave girl called Tutela promised that she would go across to the enemy with the other slave women, pretending to be their mistresses. So they dressed up as Roman mothers and girls and marched over to the enemy with a lot of people following them in tears, to make it look as though they were grieving over losing their mothers and sisters and daughters. Livius divided them up around the camp, and the slave women plied the men with lots of wine, pretending that it was a feast day for the Romans. When the men had all fallen into a deep sleep, they signalled to the Romans from a wild fig tree that stood next to the camp. The Romans attacked suddenly and were victorious. In gratitude, the senate ordered that all the slave women be freed, and gave them a financial reward too. And they decided to hold an annual sacrifice to commemorate the day, in memory of the female slaves' heroic action.

In these examples, I think you will agree, there are good reasons for not looking down with contempt on slaves, since there is ample evidence that many of them have been trustworthy, prudent and brave. Indeed, you will often find that is the kind of people who have lots of busts of their illustrious ancestors on display in their villas, and know every small twig of their family tree, who in their actions are revealed to be merely well known rather than truly noble.

The same universe is father to us all. We all trace our ancestry from this one parent, whether high- or low-born. You should not look down on any man, even if he has no idea where he comes from and Fortune seems to have abandoned him. If your ancestors include slaves and freedmen then be proud of your humble beginnings. But don't let your pride make you blind to the merits of slaves. For all slaves are capable of becoming Romans, even if it often takes several generations for this to be achieved.

But of course, if we are honest, we know that slaves can only really be expected to follow the example set by their masters. For it is hard to learn to do something well if the teacher's demonstration is bad. And if a master sets an example of carelessness, then it is difficult for the slave to learn to be careful. To be blunt, I don't think I can remember a single case of good slaves belonging to a bad master. I do, however, know of a great many bad slaves who belong to a good master, and they are punished for it. If you want to make your slaves morally better people, then you have to supervise their work, and examine it; and you have to be willing to reward those responsible for what has been done well, just as you must not be frightened to punish a slave who has acted badly. For it is only by your example and teaching that your slaves can ever be expected to improve.

Slaves are nearly always inferior to their masters and it is a sad fact that most slaves are not given the training they should be given to make them better. It is an even sadder fact of life today that we have to rely on these underlings for so many services. We use slaves to grow our food and cook it. We employ them to wash our clothes and carry our bags. I know of one great Roman who had so little self-restraint that he suffered the ultimate indignity of having to use a slave to restrain his hand from taking too much food when he was dining. How disgraceful it is that he should have been more ready to obey his slave than himself! It is masters like him, who are addicted to luxury, who are the true slaves.

·· COMMENTARY ··

Falx's attitude takes a distinctly more philosophical turn in this chapter. His writings show the influence of Stoic thinking, which affected a number of the Roman philosopher Seneca's texts on the subject of slavery. In this way of thinking, the fact that a slave is a slave is seen as irrelevant. What matters is the inner soul of the individual. It was equally possible for a wealthy owner to be the real slave if he was addicted to certain vices, such as sex or eating.

This approach to slavery was quite different from that of the classical Greeks. In Greek philosophy, such as that of Aristotle, slavery was seen as a natural opposite to the freedom of the Greeks. Barbarians and slaves were almost synonymous. Much later, in the British and American slave trade, this kind of reasoning provided a basis for a racial model of slavery which saw blacks as being naturally suited to slavery and naturally inferior to whites. The Romans never argued for such a distinction, in part because it made no sense in a society where so many freed slaves were incorporated into the citizen body. It would have been impossible to maintain a notion of the racial purity of the Romans in the face of the overwhelming fact that so many of them were descended from slaves. This also meant that Romans had no difficulties in enslaving other Italians, even though they saw these as naturally closer to them than non-Italians. By contrast, the Greeks found the idea of enslaving other Greeks abhorrent precisely because they were seen as naturally free, regardless of what kind of character each individual possessed.

Falx has a far more humane attitude towards slaves because he sees the fact of slavery as no more than a social convention. The enslaved individual is still worth something as a human being, is capable of acting with great morality, and needs to be treated with respect because of this.

But before we start seeing the Roman empire as some kind of proto-humanist institution, we must remember that there is no notion of universal human rights in such Stoic thought. It is more that the master has some vague duty to behave decently to his slaves, so long as they behave well, in order to inspire them to behave even better. One of the main motivators for this gentler attitude may have been the fear that otherwise slaves might attack their masters. There also seems to have been a near-universal assumption that even though slaves were capable of virtuous acts, it was impossible for a slave to be better than his master. Other groups, such as women slaves, were mostly not included in these moral discussions because they simply didn't register with elite philosophers.

There is no evidence that such Stoic thinking had any effect on the actual treatment of slaves. It certainly did not give rise to any ideas of abolition, or even any criticism of slavery as a social institution. Texts such as those of Seneca were theoretical and written to impress a small audience of educated thinkers. Seneca himself makes many derogatory comments about slaves in his other writings, which contradict his more benevolent views. Falx's comments may not have been reflective of the attitude of the average Roman slave owner. Even if such ideas were to be found in society more widely, there is again no evidence that it made Roman masters more gentle towards their servants. It probably makes more sense to interpret such elite thinking as a reaction to their own changed political circumstances. The fact that people of Seneca's status now had to live under emperors like Nero made it appealing to see slavery as being unimportant. All free Romans were now in effect the political slaves of the emperor.

The discussion between the Greek and the clever slave is based on Dio Chrysostom *Oration* 15. An example of the Stoic doctrine towards slaves can be seen at Epictetus *Discourses* 4.1. Cicero repeats the Stoic doctrine that masters had a duty to behave justly even towards the lowest kinds of people in *On Duties* 1.13.41. For the Roman idea that it was necessary to show your worth by your actions not by birth alone, see Dio Chrysostom *Oration* 15. The story of the Roman who used a slave to stop himself overeating is at Pliny the Elder *Natural History* 28.14. Accounts of slaves who performed great acts of virtue are listed in Suetonius *Grammarians*,

Macrobius *Saturnalia* 1.10.16–25 and Seneca *On Benefits* 3.23–8. The view that slaves should be treated as human beings is in Seneca *Letters* 47. Analysis of the various theories of slavery that existed in antiquity can be found in Peter Garnsey's *Ideas of slavery from Aristotle to Augustine*.

· CHAPTER V ·

THE PUNISHMENT OF SLAVES

W HEN YOU OWN A STUBBORN MULE, there is no point in using the fine art of rhetoric to try to persuade it to carry out your wishes. Likewise with your slaves: whatever high ideals of ownership you might strive to maintain, you will often find the philosophy of slavery of little practical benefit. However noble and diligent, inspired by your fine example, you might hope that your slaves will be, you will in reality find that you are sometimes obliged to give them forceful reminders of their low status in order to compel them to work hard on your behalf. There is no point thinking you would be better off treating them gently. Recalcitrant slaves do not understand logic. Such slaves are like animals and they respond best to the touch of the whip. In fact, you will find that the average slave's mind is constantly preoccupied with the risk of physical punishment. They even dream about it, and it is known that it is bad for a slave to dream of beef, because both straps and whips are made of ox hide. But this ever-present anxiety of theirs about corporal punishment should not worry you, their owner. Rather, you should understand that it helps to reinforce the dominance of the figure of the master in their life. A slave who always has the master at the back of his mind, whatever task he is carrying out, will be a more attentive, diligent and productive slave.

Slaves sometimes need to be punished but you should be careful not to do so excessively. Where possible, and within the constraints of maintaining discipline and authority, you should refrain from flogging a slave just because he gives you a cheeky or disrespectful answer. They are, after all, items of your property and if you harm them you are, in effect, damaging your own goods. If someone else were to injure you, you would naturally seek financial compensation from the courts. So it is also with your slaves, even if damage to a slave is worth only half that of damage to a free man.

Sadly, though, we all know people who have gone too far in their punishments. One friend of mine insists, as many do, that his slaves serve him and his family at meals in complete silence. I dined there recently and a muffled sneeze from a waiter brought a savage whipping. Another coughed when serving the soup, for which he was dragged out and beaten with rods. It was hardly relaxing, I have to say. I suspect that the moment we guests left, things really started to hot up and I'm told that any slaves who had failed to carry out their tasks perfectly, or any cook that had prepared a less than sump-tuous dish, were all made to dance. Then there is that famous story about Vedius Pollio, who invited his friend the divine emperor Augustus around for dinner. One of the host's slaves broke a valuable crystal cup, whereupon Vedius ordered the slave to be taken and thrown to the huge lampreys which he kept in his fish pond. Obviously he was just showing off to the emperor by letting him see how hard he could be. But this was savagery, not toughness. The boy escaped and ran to Augustus's feet for refuge. He begged that he be allowed to die by some other means than as fishmeal. Augustus was outraged at this novel form of cruelty. He ordered Vedius to free the slave. He then told the other slaves to bring all the crystal cups they could find and smash them in their master's presence. Vedius was instructed to fill in the fish pond and get rid of the lampreys.

We've all done it, of course. What master has not occasionally lashed out at his slaves from sheer exasperation at their uselessness? I heard of one local owner who became so mentally unbalanced that he threw his slave out of a first-floor window. And a friend of mine who got so fed up with an old slave who never did anything that he severed his hams so he would never move anywhere again. Even the emperor Hadrian once poked out a slave's eye with his pen when he was annoyed by him in some way. But allowances for anger aside, we should not be over zealous or invent new kinds of punishment to impress our guests. Are a man's bowels to be ripped apart just because one of your cups has been broken? You should try to control your moods if you can. For one thing, this is the kind of behaviour you find from freedmen who have gone on to own their own slaves. They are infamous for their brutality and are always calling for floggings and thrashings as if to compensate for their own servile origins.

I am of course talking here about domestic and privately owned slaves. Slaves who have been justly condemned by the courts to the mines as punishment for some heinous crime cannot expect to be so leniently treated. These slaves are destroyed physically and are forced to endure the most dreadful hardships. In the end, they often pray for death because of the magnitude of their suffering. These criminals deserve their fates. But one can't help feeling some sympathy for slaves who are being used by contractors to work the mines in hardly less dreadful circumstances. These men generate unbelievable wealth for their owners, but are ruined by their constant, day-and-night underground excavations. The conditions are bad, and they are not allowed to rest and are instead forced by the beatings given out by their overseers to keep working. Still, there are plenty of freeborn men who have to earn a living by working the mines. And these mines are no longer the routes to easy fortunes they once were. The silver- and gold-bearing seams have dried up and considerably more work is required in more dangerous circumstances to produce the same amount of bullion.

Nor am I talking about slaves who have been rightly sentenced by the courts to be thrown to the wild beasts in the arena for the entertainment of our citizens. None of these slaves have been sent to suffer such a fate simply on their owners' whims, since owners may not sell their slaves for such a purpose. When we see them being torn limb from limb, or we hear the crunching and grinding of bones, we may therefore relax and be certain that we are witnessing the suitable punishment of a deserving criminal. A friend of mine has recently had some most delicate and graceful mosaics showing these executions put up in his dining room, and they look splendid!

There are also certain situations when a privately owned, domestic slave should suffer the ultimate penalty. I am thinking, above all, of the occasions when a slave is able to come to their master's help, but fails to do so. For when a slave's master is in danger, the slave should have more regard for his master's safety than his own. I remember once that a slave girl was sleeping in the same bedroom as her mistress when a murderer broke in. He threatened to kill the girl if she cried out and so she kept quiet, when she could definitely have come to her mistress's assistance, either by putting her own body in the way, or by shouting loudly to alert other slaves in the household. It was only right that the girl was executed, so that other slaves did not get the idea that they could think about their own safety when their owners were in danger.

For myself, when it comes to punishing my slaves, I often rely on the services of an outside contractor. The local council here offers a service by which they will administer beatings for a set fee. The terms are very modest, about four sesterces per flogging if I remember rightly. For that they come and set up a gibbet on to which they bind the offending slave after they have solemnly led him out from the room in which he is being held. They think of everything, even supplying the ropes to tie the slave. It provides a salutary warning to the rest of the slaves to behave properly and saves you from getting your own hands dirty. In the past, when it was permissible for a master to execute his own slaves, these contractors provided a crucifixion service too, supplying both cross and nails. Hot pitch was also available where torture was required. Most masters back then would try any slave in their household who was accused of a serious crime in the presence of all the other dependants, and have the offender killed if he was found guilty.

In my country estates I keep a dingy, underground prison to punish errant slaves with a period of solitude. It has only a few slits for light at the top, which cannot be reached by hand, and the slaves are fed minimally. While this is not strictly legal these days, I find it useful to have something that can strike fear into even the most awkward and stubborn of country slaves. Or I sentence slaves to work in the mill and take the place of the mules in turning the millstones. Such hard labour can quickly sort out miscreants. They soon make a sorrowful picture: covered in rags, their heads shaved, irons clamped on their feet, sallow faces, all covered with flour from the mill, like wrestlers who get covered with fine sand when they fight. Mind you, I don't keep them at it for long, as such effort can soon become demoralising instead of inspiring the slave to work harder in his proper tasks.

You must never feel guilty at meting out such punishments. Slaves are ruined by their own wickedness, not by a master's cruelty. Incidentally, if you do suffer any pangs of conscience after hitting a slave unjustly, either with your hand or an object, I have heard it on good authority that if you immediately spit into the palm of the hand that inflicted the wound then the resentment of the victim is immediately softened. The emperor Hadrian went so far as to apologise directly to the slave whose eye he had poked out with his pen. He asked the slave what he wanted by way of recompense. But the slave just grew bold and had the temerity to say that there was nothing the emperor could do as nothing could compensate for the loss of an eye. It just goes to show that if you treat slaves too gently they will soon take advantage of your softness and grow difficult.

Be careful not to hurt your hand when striking a slave. This is especially true if you do it in anger. Some have even been known to use not just their fists but their feet on their servants, or to stab them with a knife that they happened to be holding. I know several friends who have wounded their hands by hitting their slaves in the teeth. A medical friend of mine, a worthy man in every respect, has such a temper he regularly uses his hands on his servants, and sometimes his legs too. Most of the time, though, he attacks them with a leather strap, or with any wooden object that comes to hand. He is always bruising himself and pulling muscles from his exertions, inflicting injury on the very man who should be doling it out.

We should also remember that owning slaves provides an opportunity for the owner's personal improvement. It teaches us how to control our base instincts. That is another reason why I choose not to strike slaves with my own hands. It is far better to restrain your rage for a few moments and, instead of rupturing yourself in a fit of anger, consider carefully exactly how many strokes of the rod or the whip the slave deserves to receive. This can then be carried out by another servant trained in such a task or by contractors brought in.

Pausing before punishing your slaves also gives a chance for your moral superiority to assert itself. We have, after all, forgiven the Gauls and the Britons for resisting us – why should we not show the same spirit of forgiveness to those who are even more worthless? Should we never show mercy to some miserable slave who has been lazy or talkative? If he's a child, his age should excuse him, if female, her sex. Just as we should have too much respect to grow angry with our superiors, we should have too much self-respect to grow angry with our slaves. It is hardly an act of heroism to send some wretched slave off to the prison house to cool off for a few days.

Such outbursts of uncontrolled rage can, in any case, lead to legal complications. There was once a lady called Statilia, who asked the emperor whether she had to fulfil a clause in her late husband's will, a clause that had clearly been written while he was furious with two of his slaves. The will stated that one of the slaves was to be kept chained up for ever, and the other was to be sold overseas. The emperor replied that Statilia's husband had been alive long enough after he had made the will that, if he had wanted to, he could have had it rewritten to exclude these clauses inserted in anger. So unless there was some evidence that the master's anger had in fact been assuaged by the slaves – they might perhaps have carried out some particularly meritorious act which it would be reasonable to assume would have softened their master's ire – then his last wishes should be respected. And the emperor made it clear that it would take some proper written evidence to prove this, not something like the word of another slave.

There has been a growing tendency for the emperor

to intervene in relations between masters and slaves. It is only natural that the father of the state, who is patron and head of the household to us all, should provide us with guidance on how best to manage our domestic affairs. Several emperors have decreed that a slave who appealed to the gods or to a statue of the divine emperor himself had the right to have his complaints investigated. This resulted from the fact that several provincial governors asked the emperor what they should do with slaves who took refuge in a temple or at the statues of emperors. The emperor declared that if it was the master's intolerable cruelty that had driven the slave to run away and seek refuge, then the slaves should be sold to new masters, with the proceeds of the sale going to the original owner. This was a sensible decision, since it is in the public interest that people should not use their property badly. For although the power of the master over a slave must be absolute, it is in the interests of owners in general that protection against brutality or starvation or intolerable injustice should not be denied to those who rightly appeal against them.

In the old days of the republic, the head of the household could punish their slaves as they saw fit, just as they could their sons, and could even execute them. Now such power over life has been transferred to the magistrates. No master now can act against their slaves with excessive cruelty or brutality, unless they have some legal grounds for doing so. Indeed, in accordance with a law of the divine emperor Antoninus Pius, anyone who kills his own slave without proper cause is to be punished just as severely as someone who kills another's slave.

So just to be clear, it is perfectly legal for you to chastise a slave of yours by beating him with sticks or whipping him or having him put into chains in order to keep him under guard. You will not face any criminal accusation even if the slave happens to die during the punishment. But you will be accused of murder if you willingly kill him with a stick or stone, if you inflict a lethal wound by using some form of weapon, if you have him hanged by a noose, if you have him thrown from a great height, or if you pour poison into him. You will also be prosecuted if you mutilate his body with punishments that are the preserve of the state, by which I mean the instruments of torture that I shall describe in detail in the next chapter.

One type of slave misbehaviour deserves special mention. I am talking here about runaways. Fleeing is a depressingly common problem among slaves, one that you will undoubtedly face at some time or other while you are head of the household. This will even happen when you have tried your utmost to treat your slaves fairly and decently, have given them a sufficiency of food, shelter and clothing, and punished them only when they deserved it. You will find that such malcontents will take advantage of any kind of war or insecurity to run off, hoping that people will be too distracted by other events to take any notice of their escape.

Naturally you will be keen to recover your lost property. I can recommend offering a reward for the slave's return or putting up a notice and description in the marketplace. Give relevant factual information and try to pick on a distinguishing feature of the slave that will make him easily recognisable. An example of a notice I have used reads: 'A boy called Hermon has run away, age about 15, wearing a cloak and a belt. He swaggers around as if he were someone of note, chattering in a shrill voice. Anyone who brings him back will receive three hundred sesterces; anyone who gives information that he has taken refuge at a temple will get one hundred sesterces. Please give any information you have to the Governor's officials.'

Professional slave catchers can also be called in but their fees are high. Speed is of the essence here in that they can use dogs to track down runaways who have not had time to travel far from your household. You will also want to ask the authorities to help you. Here I have often observed that it is beneficial to use your network of acquaintances to ensure that officials do their best to have the fugitive returned to you. Write to any that you know who are in authority in places where you believe runaways of yours are hiding, sending your respectful greetings and claiming the benefits of their proven friendship towards you. Request that they listen to the evidence submitted by your agent and then seek out these slaves and return them to you.

If all else fails you can resort to magic and put a spell on the runaway, although I cannot say that I recommend such superstition. A better use of your time and money would be to insure yourself against such losses.

If runaways are captured and returned to you, I recommend leniency, although many would argue otherwise. Most opt for imprisoning the slave, beating them soundly or even cutting off a limb. No doubt this is justified in many respects but there is a risk that the returned slave will be so petrified of what fate awaits him that he will kill himself.

Branding the runaway on the face offers a simpler solution for preventing them from doing it again. This method effectively makes it impossible for the slave to escape detection if he tries to run away again. Others force the slave to wear a locked metal collar, embossed with a phrase such as 'Seize me because I'm a runaway' or 'Send me back to Falx and get a reward of a gold coin.' You can generally abbreviate the first of these to simple initials, as everyone understands what it means.

If a runaway is found to have gone to a shrine to appeal to the gods for mercy you will have to go through the due process of the law. Allow the magistrate or the priest to investigate the case and decide between you and the slave. If he finds for you then you should take the slave back in good grace and swear that you will not harbour a grudge against them. If he finds against you, then so what? There is no disgrace in giving way to the divine emperor and this offers a face-saving way for you to grant the slave what he most wants – a new master – and for you to get the cost of replacing him. There will always be discontented slaves who do not appreciate all that you have done for them and it is better that there is some way for you to recoup the capital that you have spent on the ingrate. Otherwise, you lose the entire cost if the slave manages to escape successfully or dies in the attempt or is sentenced to be thrown to the beasts as a punishment by a magistrate in some far-off province where he is captured.

There is an extraordinary story about a runaway that I must tell you. I heard it from a literary friend who witnessed it himself with his own eyes in the city of Rome. One day in the Circus Maximus a huge fight between various wild beasts was being put on before the people. Hundreds of animals had been brought in for the entertainment, and these were not just harmless creatures like antelopes and giraffes but great ugly beasts that were remarkable for their colossal size and especial ferocity. Even among this terrifying menagerie, it was the lions that stood out. One lion in particular drew attention to himself because his body was so large and his demeanour so vicious. He possessed a deep and terrifying roar, a most powerful neck and a rich mane that flowed over his shoulders. Not having been fed for several days, he was clearly ravenous for flesh.

At this point, a number of prisoners who had been condemned to be thrown to the wild beasts were brought into the Circus. One of them was a slave called Androcles, who had belonged to a former consul. He was put into the ring and the great lion was released. The crowd licked their lips in anticipation of what this great lion would do to this defenceless man. But the most remarkable thing happened. When the lion saw him from a distance, rather than charge at him and devour him, he stopped before him, as if he were thunderstruck, and then approached the man slowly and quietly, as if he recognised him. Then, wagging his tail in a gentle way, as if he were some kind of fawning dog, he came right up close to the man, who was now half dead from fright, and gently licked his feet and hands. As this fierce beast delicately caressed him, Androcles slowly calmed down and composed himself, and finally managed to open his eyes and look at the lion. He clearly recognised him, his face broke out into a broad smile, and he gave the animal a big hug.

The crowd were so astonished at such an amazing sight that they started to shout loudly, wanting to know what had happened. The emperor at the time summoned Androcles to be brought before him and asked him why this fiercest of lions had spared him. And Androcles told him a strange and surprising story.

'My master,' said he, 'was governing Africa as proconsul. But he was a vicious man. And eventually I could bear his undeserved, daily floggings no more and decided to run away. In order to escape from so important a man, I took refuge in the desert, beyond the fertile plain of that region. My plan was that if I couldn't find food and water then I would kill myself rather than be sent back to him. One day, the heat of the midday sun was so scorching that I went into a secluded cave and hid myself. Soon afterwards, this lion limped into the cave. He was lame and one of his paws was bleeding profusely and he gave out great groans from the pain of his wound.

'At first I was terrified at the sight of the lion approaching. I had clearly stumbled into the lion's den and thought I was done for. But when the lion saw me cowering at a distance, he came up to me meekly, and gently lifted up his paw, as if to ask for help. I could see that a huge splinter had embedded itself in the sole of the paw and with difficulty I pulled it out. Then I squeezed out the pus that had filled the wound, wiped away the blood, and dried it thoroughly. I didn't feel at all frightened now. The lion was clearly enormously relieved at having the wound seen to. He put his paw in my hand, lay down on the floor of the cave and went to sleep. For three whole years the lion and I lived in the same cave, and we even shared the same food. For the lion used to bring me back the choicest parts of his kill, which I would dry in the midday sun, since I had no fire on which to cook them, and then eat.

'But eventually I grew tired of living in the wild. I left the cave one day when the lion had gone off to hunt. I travelled for three days but was spotted and captured by some soldiers, who took me from Africa to Rome, where my master had now returned. He immediately had me condemned to death by being thrown to the wild beasts. But clearly the lion was also captured and himself sent to Rome to play his part in the games. And now he is repaying me for the kindness I showed him in curing his paw.'

The crowd were desperate to know what Androcles was telling the emperor, so he had messengers write it out in full on placards, which were carried around the Circus. Once they knew his story, everyone demanded that he be freed. The emperor obliged and also presented him with the lion at the suggestion of the people. And for a long time after, you would see Androcles and his lion, on a thin leash, wandering round the streets of Rome, where he would be given money by admiring crowds and the lion would be sprinkled with flowers. And people would exclaim, 'This is the lion that was a man's friend, and this is the man who was doctor to a lion.'

·· COMMENTARY ··

Falx's tougher side re-emerges in this chapter. But the physical punishment of slaves by their Roman masters was normal, acceptable and routine. In Roman comedies by Plautus, for example, the typical slave is portrayed as being obsessed with avoiding the master's whip. That doesn't mean that all slaves were harshly and brutally treated. No doubt the individual slave's treatment will have varied considerably depending on the attitude of the master. The Romans themselves were critical of owners who treated their slaves with excessive severity and it is possible that this kind of communal policing by means of reputation served to restrain some masters from getting too carried away when punishing their slaves.

This public concern was eventually expressed in imperial legislation that limited the degree to which a master could punish a slave with impunity. The famous story of Vedius Pollio trying to throw one of his slave boys to his lampreys as punishment for breaking a crystal cup is recorded precisely because it was seen as an unacceptable and overly harsh form of action. The emperor Augustus's intervention in this story emphasises that imperial involvement was not primarily motivated by a desire to improve the living conditions of the slaves, but by the fact that emperors were involved in all aspects of their subjects' lives and so were expected to set and enforce acceptable standards of social behaviour.

Slaves were subject to the arbitrary whims and moods of their owner. The story of Hadrian poking his slave's eye out with his pen was probably remarkable, and so worth recording for posterity, precisely because this kind of behaviour was out of character for him. But he still did it. Yet if even a thoughtful emperor could act so callously when in a bad mood then how much more often did assaults of this kind occur among normal slave owners? What made the story even more notable for a Roman audience was that the slave grew bold when asked what he would like as recompense. It was unthinkable for a slave to be so disrespectful to his master, especially when he had taken the trouble to seek to offer some redress for the injury he had caused. The impression is given that what Hadrian is sorry for is that he lost his temper, not for what that loss of control meant for the slave. The focus was on the character of the owner not the fate of the slave.

Criminal slaves who were condemned to the mines, to work in the galleys of ships, or to be thrown to the beasts in the amphitheatre were seen as completely deserving of their fate. It is tempting to think that the Romans will have felt some pity for poor men and women being thrown to the lions, but there is little evidence for this. They seem to have regarded such punishment as just deserts for slaves who were so worthless that they could not even be good at being slaves.

Runaways were a recurrent problem for masters. The loss of capital this represented was something they sought hard to avoid. In the *Oracles of Astrampsychus*, one of the questions is of a master seeking an answer to 'Will I find the fugitive?' It is heartening to find that the odds implied by the ten possible responses favour the runaway.

The replies suggest that 60 per cent will not be found, 30 per cent will be and 10 per cent only after a time. Perhaps this is why so many slaves appear to have tried to flee: it often worked. The resources masters had to try to track down an individual in the vast expanse of the Roman empire were limited. There was no police force to help and so long as the slave managed to escape from the immediate vicinity in which he might be recognised, then there was probably a reasonable possibility of starting life afresh as a free man.

The story of Androcles and the lion here related is a later expansion of the old Aesop fable. In this Roman version it is interesting that the slave gives his own account of his motivation for running away: his brutal and unjust treatment. While this is probably a fictional story (although the writer claims to have got it from an eyewitness at the event), it does give some indication of how some slaves bristled at their dreadful treatment and were prepared to take enormous risks to their personal safety in order to achieve the possibility of living in freedom. See Keith Bradley, *Slavery and Society at Rome*, pp. 107–8.

The story of Vedius Pollio is in Dio Cassius 54.23.1. Pollio's actions are also criticised by Seneca, *On Anger* 3.40. The description of slaves being punished by working in the flour mill comes from Apuleius's novel, *The Golden Ass* 9.12. On the dreadful conditions in the mines, see Diodorus Siculus 5.36–8. The story of Statilia is in the Justinian *Code* 3.36.5. For people injuring themselves by hitting their slaves, see Galen *The Diseases of the Mind* 4. An example of a wealthy owner trying to use his contacts to get his runaways returned can be found in Symmachus *Letters* 9.140. On the right of a slave to appeal to the gods or a statue of the divine emperor, see Justinian *Institutes* 1.8.2.

CHAPTER VI

WHEN ONLY TORTURE
WILL DO

THE PUNISHMENTS I HAVE OUTLINED in the
previous chapter should enable you to maintain discipline and authority within your household. There are
times, though, when one of your slaves might become
involved with the law. On these occasions, whenever a
slave has to appear as a witness in court, it is a legal
requirement that they give their evidence under torture.
The reason for this is obvious. Slaves are habitual liars
and so it is only when they suffer pain that they can be
expected to reveal the truth. The only requirement is
that the slave's owner has willingly offered up the slave
for torture. The only exception is that the slave cannot
testify against his master, apart from in cases of treason.

Slaves themselves are for the most part morally worthless, a fact that is reflected in their extreme cowardice in
the face of fear. It is pathetic to observe their whimpers,
their voluble confessions and their terror when faced
with the implements of torture. None of which does
them any good, of course, because their evidence will

only be taken under torture. Otherwise they might say anything to get themselves, literally, off the hook. The prudence and humaneness of this course can be seen in the example of the slave Primitivus. He was so desperate to get away from his master that he even accused himself of murder and went so far as to name accomplices. It was only when he was put to the torture that the truth emerged, which was that no such crime had ever been committed. If it had not been for the torture, a slave would have been executed, innocent others would have been condemned to the mines, and a law-abiding owner would have been deprived of his property.

The torture of slaves is a common sight in the law courts. I did once hear of someone objecting to a slave being tortured. It was a case of joint ownership, of a beautiful slave girl, by two men who had then fallen out about some business affair and had a fight in which one was badly wounded. The injured party took the other to court where the accused refused to allow the torture of the slave girl because he claimed he was in love with her. Naturally, the wounded man argued that she was in the ideal position to give evidence about the matter, since she was owned equally by the two of them and was able to see who had caused the fight and who had struck the first blow. He also said that the accused's own slaves, who the accused owned outright and was happy to put up for examination, would probably just have tried to make their master happy by telling all kinds of lies about the accuser. Unfortunately, I do not recall what happened in the end.

There are several standard ways of carrying out the

torture. In the first, the slave will have his hands tied, be hung up by a rope and then flogged with a whip. Some of these whips will have tips made of sharp metal or bone that will cut into the flesh. In the second, the slave will be racked, either on a wooden frame, which is known as the 'little horse', or else placed on an implement called the 'lyre-strings', both of which are designed to use a system of weights to slowly stretch, dislocate and finally separate limb from limb. Or two heavy pieces of wood will be used to break the legs. Another method is burning. Boiling pitch, hot metal plates, or flaming torches will be applied to the slave to extract the evidence that the court requires. Finally there are the hooks, whose razor-sharp teeth are drawn across the flesh of the victim's sides. All of these procedures are carried out in public, within the courtroom.

Despite the vigour of these methods, care is taken that the slaves do not die under interrogation, although it has to be said that in practice they frequently do. And once the evidence has been obtained it has to be remembered that we are talking here about slaves. They can never be fully trusted and you should bear in mind that some will not reveal the truth but say anything just to get the torture to stop. And torture should only be used as a last resort in an investigation, at the point when someone is actually being suspected of committing a crime and no other proof from other means has been forthcoming.

I mentioned that slaves cannot be tortured for evidence against their own masters without their permission. Our divine emperor Augustus, though, set the precedent for avoiding this legal nicety. He ordered that whenever this situation should arise in an investigation, the slave in question should be forcibly sold to the public treasury or to the emperor himself, so that the slave would no longer belong to the same owner and could be interrogated in the usual way. Not surprisingly, there were some who were opposed to false sales of this type since they argued it made a mockery of the law. But others argued that it was vital for such transactions to be carried out, otherwise the many plots that were being made against the emperor under cover of this provision, and which were a constant threat to the stability of the state, might not be discovered.

The murder of a master must be given a special mention. The law states that whenever slaves are present under the same roof when the master is murdered, and they do nothing to help him escape such a fate, then they shall all be questioned under torture and then executed. The reasons for this law are obvious. First and foremost is that fact that no household could ever be safe if the slaves were not compelled to protect their master's life, whether the threat came from other household members or not, even if it meant placing their own lives at risk.

There are clearly some legal technicalities that have to be addressed here. What does the term 'under the same roof' mean? Does it mean within the walls of the house or in the same room? In fact it is generally taken to mean 'within earshot of the murder', for if the slaves were close enough to be able to hear their master's cries for help then they were also close enough to be able to offer it. Of course, some people have a louder voice than others, and some have better hearing, so it will be for the court to adjudicate on what seems reasonable in each case. Also, any last will the deceased owner had made must not be opened until the investigation is finished. Otherwise, the slaves in question might be named as beneficiaries and be freed, a freedom which would then spare them from the demands of the law for the torture of slaves.

By 'murdered' the law means all who have died as a result of violence or bloodshed, such as being strangled, thrown from a great height, or being hit with a blunt object or other such weapon. But if the master has been secretly poisoned then this law does not apply. For the purpose of this law is to ensure that slaves lend assistance to their master when it is clear that he needs it most. Since they cannot be expected to know that their master was being surreptitiously poisoned, they could not have prevented it from happening (and, in this case, other laws will take vengeance for the master's death on those who were responsible for it). But the law does apply if the poison was being administered by force.

If the master commits suicide then this law does not apply and the slaves under the same roof should not be tortured and executed. But if the owner has turned his hand against himself within sight of his slaves and they could have prevented him from doing so, then the law will apply and they will be punished. If they were not able to help, then they will be acquitted.

The divine emperor Hadrian decreed that the law should certainly be applied to those in the same room as the murder victim. He also stated that no mercy should be shown to slaves who had failed to act simply out of fear of being killed themselves, and that slaves must assist their owners in some way, if only by just shouting for help from others. However, he conceded that if the murder happened to have taken place when the master was out in his country estate, where a cry might carry for a great distance, then it would be highly unjust if all the slaves in his property were to be tortured and punished. In his great mercy, the emperor decreed that it was sufficient to interrogate only those slaves who were with their master when he was killed and are suspected of having either carried it out or having been accomplices. If the master was travelling and happened to be alone, then the law does not apply. Slave boys who are children and slave girls who are not yet of marriageable age should also not be tortured, since some allowance should be made for their youth.

If there is perhaps an objection to the use of evidence obtained from slaves, it is not that it has been obtained via torture – which is necessary for there to be any possibility that the truth might emerge – but that it comes from men who are generally morally worthless. This is certainly the case when their evidence is put against that of free men. It hardly seems right that the words of a slave should be believed instead of those of a free man. Moreover, slaves will certainly have done many wicked things in their lives whereas the free man will have done his best to serve the state in a variety of capacities.

It is true that in the past some owners went too far in torturing their slaves in order to try to force them to reveal the so-called truth. A woman called Sassia was once trying to fabricate evidence that her son Cluentius had murdered his stepfather, Oppianicus. She therefore tortured three slaves, whose names were Strato, Ascla and Nicostratus, but they withstood the ordeal. Not a woman to be resisted, she tried again, using tortures of the most exquisite cruelty. Witnesses were unable to bear the sight. In the end even the torturer was worn out. Furious, Sassia demanded that the torturer press on but one of the witnesses complained that he feared the interrogation was now being performed not so much to discover the truth as to make the slaves say something untrue. The other witnesses agreed and together they left. But she continued to pursue the slaves. Eventually, the slave Nicostratus died, and she had Strato crucified after having his tongue cut out to prevent him from incriminating her.

In those days, Sassia had every right to torture her slaves to help her find out the truth of what had happened. But she pursued them with a vigour that would no longer be permitted now that our great emperors have chosen to involve themselves in the relations between a master and his slaves. As we have seen, masters can no longer just kill their slaves for no good reason. Slaves have the right to appeal to a magistrate and also have rights of asylum against abusive masters. And as I've mentioned before, they can also take refuge before a statue of the emperor.

Most shockingly, even one of our own emperors abused the use of torture to obtain evidence from slaves to secure the condemnation of their masters. So Domitian, whenever he wished to fill up the state coffers and line his own pocket, would target certain super-rich individuals. But finding himself unable to secure their prosecution in legal ways, he would charge them with high treason. He would then torture the household slaves (for which he did not need the master's permission because of the severity of the charge), to ascertain so-called facts about their owner's anti-imperial conspiracies. In fact, he often did not bother with the torture. He just encouraged and bribed the slaves to reveal what their masters had allegedly been up to. In doing so, he did in fact reveal that he had no better morals than a slave himself.

·· COMMENTARY ··

The routine torture of slaves in legal proceedings is, to the modern reader, one of the most shocking abuses. But the Romans saw such treatment as completely normal. Slaves were too unimportant and morally weak to be relied upon to tell the truth. Torture was seen simply as a way of getting at the truth and so was both sensible and served the cause of justice. The fact that slaves had few legal rights meant that they were liable to the roughest kind of treatment. In fact, their lack of social status was seen as requiring rough treatment to make sure that they acted properly and told the truth.

The Romans did realise that evidence obtained under torture needed to be treated with caution. Plenty of examples attest to slaves lying to get the pain to stop. But such examples did not, in their eyes, reduce the benefit of the practice as a whole. Also, the Romans did not resort to torture lightly. It was used in the later stages of a criminal investigation once it had been established that a crime had been committed and there was insufficient alternative evidence to gain a conviction by other means.

The laws concerning the murder of masters by slaves were especially harsh. Killing all those who were present generated intriguing legal questions but also made sure that household slaves had a vested interest in revealing any kind of plot that other slaves might have been hatching under the same roof. It also made sure that slaves were more likely to come to their master's aid in any attack on him. Examples of master-murder are actually remarkably rare in the surviving Roman sources. It is hard to know how this should be interpreted. It might suggest that master-slave relations were not as conflictual as we might imagine. Or maybe it simply reflects the fact that the brutal laws successfully terrorised the servile population into leaving their owners well alone. Or it might be that our sources only record a few celebrated cases, when in reality master-murder was more common, especially among the non-elite population.

Slaves owners had once had the right to treat their slaves as they wished, which included torturing them. The story about Sassia shows that some went to extremes, even though this episode is recorded because of its uniqueness. Various emperors restricted this right so that masters had to justify their actions. Slaves were also given the legal right of appeal against abusive treatment. In common with other imperial legislation concerning slaves, this should probably not be interpreted as emperors wishing to improve the conditions of the servile population. As emperors came to be more and more involved in all aspects of life, people simply looked to them to give guidance on what limits there should be in the treatment of slaves.

The laws about the torture of slaves can be found in *Digest* 48.18. The legal discussion about the technicalities of which slaves should be executed when their master is murdered can be found in *Digest* 29.5. On the restriction of the rights of owners to execute slaves, see *Digest* 18.1.42 and *Theodosian Code* 9.12.1. For Augustus circumventing the restriction against torturing slaves to give evidence against their masters, see Dio Cassius 55.5. On the torture of slaves even to incriminate their masters in cases of treason, see *Theodosian Code* 9.6. The story of a lover wanting to spare his jointly owned slave from torture comes from Lysias 4. The story of Sassia is in Cicero's speech *In Defence of Cluentius*.

CHAPTER VII

FUN AND GAMES

A SLAVE'S FATE IS TO WORK. It is a life of toiling to keep his master happy. The slave must be ever watchful to the needs of his master, his family or his representatives. But being a slave is not all sweat and labour. It is only right that there should be some time for relaxation and silly entertainments. This is prudent, if only to ensure that your slaves maintain their morale and so can carry out their hard work. For a contented slave is a productive slave. Conversely, those slaves who have sunk into misery will hang about aimlessly, always trying to shirk the work that has been allotted to them. Or they will just whinge constantly. It is the festival of the Saturnalia that gives them the best opportunity to let off steam.

The Saturnalia date back to ancient history, but they celebrate the time when Saturn ruled the world in a golden age of equality. Then neither rank nor social hierarchy existed. Slavery and even private property were unknown, and all men owned everything in common.

The festival starts on 17 December and lasts for several days. In olden times, one single day was deemed sufficient but now, in our age of leisure and softness, greater licence is permitted. It is a time of great excitement and you will find all Rome at fever pitch. A public feast is held at the temple of Saturn and shouts of 'Io Saturnalia' fill the air. The common people get carried away. They go around revelling, singing frivolous and obscene songs, doing so even in the streets and the marketplaces, which would on a normal day be a practice that would signal disgrace and ridicule for a rich man and insanity for a poor man. Their feasting is dissolute and their dancing licentious. The feast reflects the fact that this is a time of plenty for all, not just the elite whose jaws are always at Saturnalia. This is more than a mere holiday. It is when the whole world is turned upside down. All that is normally seen as good behaviour is reversed, so that it is seen as proper to be blasphemous, coarse, dirty and drunken. There are spectacles held in the theatres and amphitheatres, pageants in the streets, and comic shows in the marketplace. A whole range of itinerant entertainers, jugglers and snake charmers fill the forum. People go about telling jokes about the city officials. The crowd ridicules everything, including the gods, and even mocks the emperor, swearing and laughing at his statues.

People show off their party clothes and wear brightly coloured tunics instead of the toga. And they put on the felt cap that is usually worn by freedmen, to symbolise the licence of the occasion and the abolition of hierarchy. Even the emperor does. Everyone exchanges presents, as would usually be done only between equals. Gambling is permitted. Even a timid home-bred slave is not afraid to look straight at the Aedile and shake the dice-box in his face. Slaves cannot be punished and they can even sound off at their masters. Indeed, it is your job as master to wait on them at table at the Saturnalia feast. Extra wine is allotted to the household. Men dress up as women. The slaves will elect a mock king for the evening, and he will put on a crown and cloak, and give everyone ridiculous orders: 'ride about on the cook as if on horseback', or 'everyone drink three fingers of wine'.

How you take part yourself is up to you. One of my friends is an utter killjoy and, while the festivities are in full swing, he takes himself off to a quiet room to escape the noise emanating from the household party. He says that he finds it delightful to sit there during the Saturnalia, when all the rest of the house rings with the merry riot that is going on in the dining room, and with the shouts of the festival-makers. He says that this is best, because then he does not interfere with their fun and they do not feel restrained in any way. Above all, he says that it means they do not distract him from his studies.

What a bore! I feel it is far better to throw yourself into the spirit of things. You will be amazed at how much goodwill it generates among the slaves if you do. What I do is drink and get drunk, shout, play games and throw dice, sing stark naked, clap and shake my belly, and sometimes even get pushed head first into cold water with my face smeared in soot. The household loves it.

It is complete madness. It is a world where all the cornerstones of the normal structure of society are inverted: male and female, master and slave, are all the opposite of what you expect them to be. It lets the slaves create an image of life as they no doubt want it to be. It is also a world where the beauty of classical form is replaced with the grotesque. Everything is brought down to a base level and the dinner reverberates with loud farting and swearing. They even make rude gestures at each other and show no deference to anyone. They throw things about and you should make sure that only your cheapest crockery is used. In some places they even torture animals for entertainment.

Sex is everywhere, you will not be surprised to hear. No doubt it is all meant to symbolise fertility and abundance but nowadays it is simply an opportunity for the young to indulge in excessive and lewd behaviour. Out in the streets you will find tumultuous processions and the marketplace filled with men leering at the women and making unseemly suggestions to them. And when night falls, no one sleeps. The common people carry on singing, and engaging in wild dancing, and mocking jokes. They do this even in the commercial district, barging in, pounding on doors, shouting and swearing, ridiculing everyone they find. They make it impossible to sleep. And some people are angry with them and the things they say. But others think you should just laugh with them and certainly no one is so uptight that he thinks the festival should be banned. Even the most self-controlled individuals burst out laughing at some of the antics.

Everybody in the crowd joins in with gusto, delighting at being able to poke fun at people who they must normally treat with respect. You sometimes even find people dressing up in the processions through the street as some of the gods or as satyrs. They walk along making extraordinary, ridiculous gestures that seem to mimic and mock the mannerisms of certain well-known people. I saw one carnival procession where the people impersonated monsters, or they dressed in animal skins. Unnatural deformities, such as a calf with two udders, and dwarves, were put on show alongside them. There is something quite distasteful and even shocking about some of these processions and there are some masters who ban members of their household from attending them, although I think that is a step too far.

It is certainly true that the festival spirit does very occasionally spill over into the real world in protests and rioting. But perhaps it is simply inevitable that such high jinx will sometimes get out of hand. For if we think about the Saturnalia, it is an alternative world that is controlled by the authorities. The reign of the Saturnalian king is brief and its egalitarian spirit dies with him when he is killed in a mock ritual at the end of the festival. There are those who are of the opinion that the festivals threaten the authorities and social stability. They argue that it gives hope of revenge and future justice. In reality, I think they are simply fun holidays, mere opportunities for the people to let off a bit of steam without really changing anything. In fact, they serve to emphasise how we expect the norms of behaviour to be observed throughout the rest of the year. People do not often take advantage of the licence of the period to voice complaints against those in authority. Indeed, when at one festival, a madman seized Caesar's crown and put it on, he caused such outrage that he was lynched. Instead, the Saturnalia reinforces the social hierarchy by underlining what a temporary period of transgression and relief this is. You see this in the way that the Saturnalia reconciles citizens with other citizens who have been quarrelling and often settles family feuds. It is a release of the tensions that build up in normal life. Society works better as a result, if only because we have seen how ridiculous and chaotic the world would be if we did not have normal rules. To believe otherwise would be hopelessly optimistic. It would be like saying that because men sometimes dressed as women during the show that women were as a result raised up to positions of authority in normal life. No. The Saturnalia teaches all of us, slaves above all, how stupid and impossible it would be to change the existing order of things, because the result would be a foolish mess.

What is more important is that the day after the festival is over no sense of this party spirit be permitted to continue. I advise you to put on your sternest countenance the following morning. It is often a good time to make an example of a laggard slave, perhaps one who has taken a little too much advantage of the freedom offered by the previous day to offend you in some way.

Once normality has returned, however, I believe it is beneficial to remain on friendly terms with your slaves wherever possible and within the constraints required to maintain authority and respect. I tend to talk with some familiarity with my country slaves, provided that they have behaved themselves properly. I have observed over many years that their unending toil is lightened by such friendliness on the part of the master. Occasionally I even share a joke with them and, on still rarer occasions, allow them to joke more freely too. I do not recommend taking this approach with urban slaves, however. Their lot is far easier and they will only seek to carry on the familiarity into the many contacts you have with them in your daily life. This can only breed contempt and result in a loss of authority.

I do make an exception with my old childhood tutor, who, remarkably, is still alive although he must be well into his seventies. Given I was under his control as a boy, even though I was free and he a slave, it seems futile of me to try to treat him with a stern face. He can always remember some amusing habit I had as a child or can tell stories of how I used to risk the cane to bunk off lessons. It reminds me of how the greatest conqueror the world has ever known, Alexander the Great, was once as a boy told off by a slave. Alexander was heaping piles of enormously expensive incense on to an altar, and his tutor Leonides told him that he would only be able to afford to invoke the gods in such a lavish way once he had conquered the peoples who produced frankincense. So when Alexander had indeed won control over Arabia, he sent a whole ship laden with incense to Leonides, telling him to worship the gods unstintingly.

As for slaves' relaxation once they have returned to the normal routine, I allow them two hours rest in the evening, after their meal. I grant them only a modest amount of wine to prevent disturbances and arguments.

I recommend that you do not allow your slaves to join one of those lower-class clubs. Although they are ostensibly burial clubs with the peaceable purpose of providing enough money for a good funeral, it is to be remembered that societies of this sort have greatly disturbed the peace of many towns. For whatever name we give them, and for whatever purposes they may seemingly be founded, they will not fail to form themselves into political assemblies, however short their meetings may be, which will be used to foment unrest.

Nor should you, under any circumstances, allow your urban slaves to get into the habit of wandering into the city centre and hanging about aimlessly. Before you know it, they will be part of that lazy and sleepy-headed group of slaves who have grown accustomed to idling, to hanging about the Campus Martius, the Circus Maximus, and the theatres, to gambling, to wasting their time in the bars and taverns, and to debauching themselves in brothels. And even if you forcibly manage to bring them back to their old habits, they will never stop dreaming of such follies.

·· COMMENTARY ··

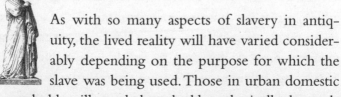

As with so many aspects of slavery in antiquity, the lived reality will have varied considerably depending on the purpose for which the slave was being used. Those in urban domestic households will mostly have had less physically demanding jobs than those employed to work the fields. But urban slaves probably also had greater opportunities to have some rest and recreation, because the city provided a far wider array of potential leisure activities than did a rural estate. Domestic slaves were less well supervised than slaves who worked in gangs in the country and so are likely to have been able to snatch some periods of respite even if it was not permitted to them. Agricultural slaves will have had the greatest need for recuperation but their ability to enjoy it will have depended on the attitude of their master. Some masters, particularly at times of slave surplus after large conquests, seem to have been content to work their slaves to death, presumably because they were cheap and expendable. These periods were not the norm in Roman society and slaves for the most part represented a significant financial investment on the part of their master. This status as a valuable asset probably meant that most owners of rural slaves would have sought to ensure that their servants received sufficient rest to enable them to recover properly from their exertions and prepare them for their next day's labour.

The festival of the Saturnalia was an annual party that clearly gave many slaves a period of significantly enhanced freedom. Domestic slaves probably benefited most from this since their direct relationship with the master and his family meant they would be given tangible rewards for their work throughout the year. There are numbers of ancient references to the Saturnalia that mention how exuberant the festival was, a bit like a Mardi Gras celebration. Whether the reality was quite as raucous as this is impossible to say. Pliny's description of how he used to hide away in his office during the festival to avoid the noisy party and make sure he did not

spoil the fun may well have been a common experience
in the larger households. Many slaves will have felt too
inhibited to speak freely to their masters and everyone
will have felt too uncomfortable with role reversals to
allow the master to wait at table. But we don't know if
that was generally the case, since Pliny was a far from
average master. He was rich and also a scholar who was
keen to distance himself from what he saw as common
entertainments. Rome was in many ways a fairly unso-
phisticated pre-industrial society and when it partied
it partied hard. As for field slaves, it is easy to imagine
that the best they will have experienced was some extra
rations and a plentiful supply of wine.

Whatever the reality of the Saturnalia, it is true that
normality nearly always returned afterwards. There are
only a few cases of the festivities getting out of hand and
resulting in riots and other displays of lower-class discontent. Slaves certainly don't seem to have tried taking
advantage of the momentary relaxation of the rules to
advance their cause in any more forceful way.

Brief references to the goings-on of the Saturnalia
can be found in Martial *Epigrams* 14.1, Seneca *Letters* 18,
Lucian *Saturnalia*, Augustine *Sermon* 198.1, Tacitus *Annals*
13.15, Epictitetus *Discourses* 1.25.8 and Libanius *Oration*
9.5–6. For the killjoy Pliny, forced to take himself off to
a quiet room to escape the noise emanating from the
household party, see his *Letters* 2.17.24. A discussion of
the Saturnalia and lower-class leisure in general can be
found in Chapter 3 'The World Turned Bottom Up' of
my book *Popular Culture in Ancient Rome*.

· CHAPTER VIII ·

REMEMBER SPARTACUS!

'YOU HAVE AS MANY ENEMIES as you have slaves.' And even if it is us who have made them enemies, as a slave owner you must keep this traditional saying constantly at the back of your mind. For no matter how trustworthy and loyal your slaves might appear to be, they would nearly all jump at the chance of being free. If you give them that chance, you might find that they will take it. And you will be the loser.

The great mass of slaves in our society is like an unexploded volcano, waiting like Vesuvius to erupt and destroy our great Roman civilisation. Their conditions are not always as fair as they should be and they harbour grudges for the defeats and perceived indignities they have suffered at our hands. You should not be surprised, therefore, to find that many slaves will carry out many acts of resistance against your authority. Some of these are major and threatening, others far more minor and merely annoying. Let me outline some of these risks in order that you can guard against them.

Slave rebellions have been mercifully rare but were none the less shocking for that. The first slave insurrections took place shortly after the second war with Carthage, which had left the Roman state tired and exhausted by long years of fighting. Not only that, but we had as a result of our ultimate victory huge numbers of slaves in our possession in Italy and Sicily who had not yet been sold off into households. Perhaps most dangerous of all was the fact that these slaves shared the same ethnic background and so were able easily to communicate, incite and conspire with each other. Even then, if they had stayed a leaderless rabble that need not have mattered too much. But their former military officers were also among them and so were able to lead them when given an opportunity to revolt.

Few civil wars have been so great as that of the slaves in Sicily. Cities were ruined, countless men died, women and children suffered the greatest misfortunes, and the whole island nearly fell to runaway slaves. These rough slaves wanted only to trash the place, and targeted the free population in particular as if to get revenge for their servitude. Most of the inhabitants were shocked at this outbreak of rebellion, but a look at the background will show that it did not arise without due cause. Sicily was a prosperous island, whose inhabitants enjoyed the benefits of its abundant harvests. People grew more rich and arrogant in equal measure. Luxury spread. As a result, they treated their slaves worse and worse, and this maltreatment made the slaves increasingly angry with their masters. At the same time, the great landowners bought up whole consignments of slaves to work on their estates.

Some were bound with chains, and many were worn out by the hard labour they were forced to do. All were branded with humiliating marks on their foreheads.

Such a huge number of slaves flooded the whole of Sicily that those who heard about it thought it had been exaggerated and did not believe it. The landowners' arrogance grew to such an extent that, rather than give their herdsmen food, they told them to steal it from others. These men were therefore compelled by their lack of provisions into dangerous raids, and crimes of this sort started happening all over the island.

At first, they attacked people who were travelling alone or in pairs in particularly isolated places. Then they banded together in groups and attacked farms in the middle of the night. They plundered them of their possessions and killed any who resisted. They grew ever bolder. Sicily became unsafe to travel in and even unsafe to live in outside of the cities. Everywhere was blighted by violence and robbery and murder. The herdsmen were used to living in the open and carrying weapons and increasingly acted as if they were bands of soldiers. The great quantities of milk and meat which were available for them to eat had the effect of dehumanising their minds and bodies, as such foods are known to do, turning them into wild animals. The entire island, therefore, came to be occupied by scattered groups of armed wild slaves. The governors wanted to control them but they were in the pay of the major landowners and so dared not move against the slaves. They were forced to overlook the fact that the province was being plundered.

The slaves who worked the land were in the meantime

exhausted by their hardships and by the unjustified and humiliating beatings they frequently suffered. In the end they could take no more. They gathered together when they got the chance and discussed how they could rebel, with their officers making detailed plans. Their leader, though, was not one of their own, but a strange Syrian, from Apamea. He was known as a magician and could carry out the most amazing miracles. He pretended that he could tell the future because the gods spoke to him when he was asleep, and many people believed him as he put on a very good act. He even pretended to have visions of the gods while awake, saying that he could hear directly from them what was going to happen.

He was also lucky in that some of the many fantasies he invented happened to come true. His reputation therefore spread and he was widely acclaimed throughout the island. In the end, he got so into his role that he would produce fire and flame from his mouth while in a trance, and would then produce divinely inspired utterances about the future. He managed to do this by means of a trick, whereby he put some fire and fuel inside a walnut in which holes had been drilled. Then he would place the walnut in his mouth without anyone seeing and would produce sparks and flames as he spoke.

Before the revolt started he proclaimed that a Syrian goddess had appeared to him and revealed that he was going to be a king. And once the revolt had taken hold, his prediction did indeed come true and he became leader of tens of thousands of slaves united in their hatred of their vicious masters and bent on destroying them.

But this first slave rebellion was as nothing compared

with that great revolt led by Spartacus. These renegades had no desire to set up their own kingdom, but simply wanted to return to their own tribes in the distant north with as much plunder as they could take with them. But as in Sicily it was the excessive brutality of slave owners that provided the spark for the revolt.

The rebellion began when a man called Lentulus Batiatus was keeping some slaves at Capua. Many of them were Celts and Thracians and they were being forced to fight as gladiators, not because they had done anything wrong, but because of the wickedness of their owner. Two hundred of them therefore decided to run away, but someone informed against them. Extra guards were brought in and only seventy-eight managed to escape, by snatching up some axes and spits from a kitchen and forcing their way out of the barracks in which they were imprisoned. Soon after they happened to come across some carts carrying gladiators' armour and weapons to another city, which they took to arm themselves.

Spartacus emerged as their leader. He was a Thracian from a nomadic tribe, who was not only very brave and physically powerful, but also more intelligent and more humane than one would expect of someone whom fortune had made a slave. You might almost have mistaken him for a Greek. The story goes that when he was first brought to Rome to be sold, a snake appeared and wound itself round his face as he was asleep, and his wife, who came from the same tribe and was a prophetess, stated that it signified that he would achieve great power and success. He led his group of runaways to the top of Mount Vesuvius, from where he launched raiding parties.

He gained further popularity with his men because he divided the booty equally and his fame attracted many new recruits from the slave estates in the area.

Their first fight was a minor skirmish with some soldiers sent out from Capua. Easily defeating them, they took their weapons too. As they travelled through the countryside they were joined by more and more slaves who saw a chance to regain their freedom and return home. Their number grew so large that the praetor Clodius was sent out from Rome against them with three thousand men. Catching up with them, he besieged them on a mountain. There was only one narrow and difficult way up this mountain, which Clodius had guarded. Everywhere else there were sheer cliffs which offered no foothold. But the slaves made ladders out of the wild vines that grew at the summit and used these to climb down the steep cliffs. The fugitives were then able to surround the Roman force, which was completely unaware of what had happened. The attack threw the Roman troops into such disorder that they fled in panic.

The second general to be sent out against them was Publius Varinus. Spartacus first defeated his deputy Furius who was accompanied by two thousand soldiers. He then defeated another deputy, Cossinus, inflicting heavy casualties and capturing more equipment. The general himself finally deigned to march against Spartacus but was unable to defeat him in a number of engagements. After each victory, Spartacus burnt any equipment he didn't need and killed all the prisoners and slaughtered the pack animals so that his army would not be impeded in any way.

But Spartacus was, as I have said, an intelligent man. He did not believe for one moment that he could break the power of the Romans even though his army now numbered seventy thousand. He knew what the outcome must therefore be: defeat and death. His only hope was to escape from Roman territory. So he led his army north towards the Alps, where they planned to cross the mountains, so each could then return to his own homeland, whether Thrace, Gaul or Germany. But his troops were enjoying themselves and their victories too much, and had become intoxicated with booty. Their arrogance and overconfidence had grown with their numbers, and they now thought themselves invincible. They therefore refused to follow their leader and instead marched all over Italy causing great devastation.

The senate was by now less concerned at the humiliation that the revolt represented than with the panic it was causing. They sent out both the consuls, as they would usually only do in a difficult and great war. One of them, Gellius, attacked the German contingent of Spartacus's army, which had greedily gone off on its own in search of plunder, and completely destroyed it. The other consul, Lentulus, surrounded Spartacus with a large army, but Spartacus again managed to win in battle. Next, Cassius, the governor of Cisalpine Gaul, confronted him with ten thousand men as he was pushing his way forward towards the Alps. Another great battle took place, and another Roman army was defeated.

The senate was now growing angry. At first the Romans had laughed off the war because it was only against gladiators and slaves, but it was now in its third

year and causing much damage. They recalled the
consuls and appointed Rome's richest man, Crassus, to
take command of the war. He sent his deputy Mummius
with two legions to follow Spartacus from a distance,
giving him strict instructions not to offer battle. But
Mummius could not help himself, since it was only a
mass of slaves that was confronting him, and he too suffered the same ignominious defeat as various Romans
before him. Casualties were heavy and many legionaries
could only save themselves by running away without
their weapons. When Crassus rearmed these troops, he
made them solemnly swear that they would not lose their
weapons again, for it was equipment such as this that was
the lifeblood to Spartacus's revolt. And to restore discipline, he reintroduced the ancient practice of decimation.
The first five hundred of the Roman escapees, who had
shown the greatest cowardice, were divided into fifty
groups of ten and one man from each, who had been
chosen by lot, was executed by being clubbed to death
by the other nine. The legionaries therefore understood
that they had more to fear from Crassus than from a
defeat at the hands of the enemy.

With their backbones thus straightened, Crassus led
his men against Spartacus. But Spartacus retreated, with
the aim of crossing to Sicily where he was confident
of gaining great support from the many slaves there.
Unable, however, to secure ships to take him, Spartacus
was eventually cornered in the toe of Italy. Crassus cut
off the end of the toe, as it were, with a wall to prevent
Spartacus from either escaping or getting supplies. It
was a vast undertaking but in remarkably quick time a

three-hundred-stade-long ditch was built right across the peninsula, which was fifteen feet wide and of equal depth. Behind the ditch was erected a high and strong wall.

At first Spartacus was not worried about the wall. But once opportunities for plunder dried up along with his supplies, his slaves became restless and he realised he would have to break out. So he waited for a stormy winter night, when it was snowing, and by secretly filling in the ditch with soil and branches managed to escape with about a third of his force. First, though, he had a Roman prisoner crucified in the area between the two armies to hammer home what would happen to them if they were defeated.

Crassus decided he would first attack those who were now fighting by themselves. He sent six thousand troops into battle, who in the most terrible combat killed over twelve thousand slaves. A sure sign of the toughness of the attack was that only two of the slaves were found with wounds on their backs. The rest had all died facing the Romans. Such was their hatred of their masters and the determination with which they were prepared to fight to the end instead of running away.

Spartacus, however, inflicted yet another defeat on one of Crassus's deputies. But this success was to prove the end of Spartacus. For it made the slaves utterly over-confident. They refused to obey orders, were keen to join battle with the Romans and gave up all thought of escaping from Italy. They forced Spartacus to march towards Crassus. His men started attacking the Roman encampment on their own initiative and, as more and more piled in, a battle grew up of its own accord.

Spartacus saw that he had no option but to bring up his whole army in battle order. He himself pushed through the melee towards Crassus but was unable to get to him. In the end, the men with him turned and fled, and he stood, all alone, surrounded by great numbers of our soldiers. He was killed while resisting arrest. The rest of his army broke ranks, and there was much slaughter. So many were killed that it was impossible to count them. Spartacus's corpse could not be found. After various mopping-up operations, about six thousand slaves had been captured, the rest having been killed. These were crucified along the length of the road from Capua to Rome. Crassus was unable to request a triumph since to do so would have been dishonourable and demeaning given that he had only defeated a band of slaves.

We can be thankful that our vigorous suppression of these early rebellions has meant that there has not been a recurrence for many decades. Yet we do still suffer the occasional small revolt. Most often these seem to be the work of a charismatic figure who manages to inspire and deceive slaves into following him. Or else it happens that a group of herdsmen get out of control and start to raid local towns and farms. Whatever the cause, it creates a great disturbance among us slave owners, who are unable to rest quite so easily at night for fear that we might come under attack ourselves.

One such uprising took place in Italy during the time of Augustus. A man called Titus Curtisius, who had once served in the praetorian guard, went about inciting the wild country slaves who worked as herdsmen in remote cattle pastures to seize their freedom. He did this first by holding secret meetings at Brundisium and neighbouring towns, then by openly distributing pamphlets to the herdsmen. But, by chance, three ships from our navy happened to put in to port there at the same time that the quaestor, whose responsibility it was to police the cattle trails, was in town. He organised the sailors from the ships and marched against the uprising, and managed to quickly suppress it just as it was about to get going properly. Even though the threat had been dealt with, the emperor sent a large force to bring the leader back to Rome for punishment. This was because Rome was already in a state of terror: the great number of domestic slaves was increasing all the time, while the free population was steadily shrinking, making people very nervous that they were vulnerable to a slave revolt.

On another occasion, in the time of Septimius Severus, Italy was terrorised by a powerful brigand called Bulla Felix. It is not certain whether he was a slave or not. He got together a band of about six hundred men and spent two years raiding and plundering parts of Italy under the very noses of the emperor and his soldiers. Even though many men were sent against him he never seemed to be where he was meant to be, was never found when found, never caught when caught, because he was both clever and bribed generously. He acquired information about everyone that was setting out from Rome and everyone that was putting into port at Brundisium, both who they were and how many they numbered, and what possessions they had with them. With most of these people, Bulla merely took a part of what they had taken with them on their journey and then let them go immediately.

He detained artisans for a time so that he could make use of their skills, but would then send them on their way with a reward for their work.

One time, when two of his men had been captured and were about to be thrown to the wild beasts, he visited the keeper of the prison, pretending that he was the governor of his native district. He claimed that he needed some men who had been condemned to carry out some terrible jobs and the jailer handed over Bulla's two men. Another time he went up to the centurion who was leading the hunt for Bulla while pretending to be somebody else. He promised the centurion that he would show him where Bulla was hiding so long as he followed him. Then, when he agreed, Bulla led him to a remote overgrown valley where his men captured him. Later that day, he dressed up like a magistrate, summoned the centurion, and ordered that his head be shaved. He then said to him, 'Take this message to your masters: "Feed your slaves and then they won't have to become bandits."'

In fact there were a large number of imperial freedmen in Bulla's group, who were there either because they had been badly paid or not paid at all. You see, even the emperor can behave irresponsibly towards his slaves sometimes. The emperor was furious when he was told about these various events, particularly because he was winning great wars in far-off Britain but was unable to beat a simple bandit at home in Italy. Eventually he sent a military tribune from his own bodyguard and a great many horsemen to deal with Bulla, warning the tribune that dire punishments would await him if he returned empty-handed. So the tribune, after he had found out that the brigand was having an affair with another man's wife, persuaded her through her husband to help them in return for a promise of immunity from prosecution. As a result, the robber was arrested while he was asleep in a cave. He was brought before the prefect, Papinian, who asked him, 'Why did you become a robber?' And Bulla replied: 'Why are you a prefect?' Later, he was sentenced to be thrown to the wild beasts in the arena and his band was easily broken up, to such an extent did the strength of the whole six hundred lie in him.

The lesson we can really learn from these, thankfully rare, episodes of slave revolt and insurrection is that it is when we masters fail in our duty of care so that the slave is left starving or brutally treated that the slave has little option but to take active measures to improve his situation. I suspect that many of these failures occurred in the past when our great conquests made slaves as cheap as olives. When no financial input has to be made what incentive is there for an owner to take care of his investment? But now, when slaves are everywhere dear, they become dear to their masters who embrace them as part of their household.

But if the danger of our slaves revolting collectively has diminished, you should still be alert to the risk of being murdered by those whom you own yourself. Let me tell you of the prefect of Rome, Pedanius Secundus, a powerful man who nonetheless was murdered by a mere slave. It is unclear why the slave was bent on revenge. It was either because Pedanius had reneged on a deal to free him or because the slave had fallen in love with one of his master's young boys and could not bear to share his lover with him. Whatever the reason, kill him he did. So according to the ancient law, all of Pedanius's household slaves were condemned to death because they had failed to save him. For surely one of them must have known something, or suspected it, or could have intervened to prevent it from happening?

Pedanius was a wealthy man and owned four hundred domestic slaves. As this great procession was being led to their execution, the Roman people thronged the streets trying to prevent it from taking place. They went so far as to besiege the senate house. Even some senators were against the mass execution because they felt it was too harsh. But most senators argued that no change in ancient practice should be permitted. If a man of Pedanius's standing could be killed by the treason of a slave then what safety could there be for anyone unless it was made painfully clear to all slaves that their own lives were at risk if they did not protect their masters'? No doubt many innocent lives would be lost. But all great examples are marked with something of injustice about them. But it is an injustice that is compensated for by the benefit the example brings to the whole community.

Many senators still refused to agree, saying that so many of the slaves were young and female that it was inhumane to kill them all. But sense prevailed and those advocating execution won. The crowd, though, were outraged and prevented the decision from being carried out. In the end, the emperor had to line the road with troops along which the condemned slaves were marched to their deaths. One particularly conservative senator suggested that even Pedanius's freedmen who had been present under the same roof should be deported from Italy. But the emperor vetoed this measure, in case excessive cruelty aggravated a primitive custom which mercy had failed to soften.

Another case of master-murder that you should bear in mind was that of the former praetor, Larcius Macedo. He suffered a horrible fate at the hands of his slaves. Admittedly, he was an arrogant and brutal master, perhaps in part because his own father had been a slave and he wished to stamp out the stigma from his memory. One day he was having a bath in his villa when suddenly a group of his slaves surrounded him. One of them grabbed him by the throat, another hit him in the face, another in the chest and stomach, another – would you believe it – in the groin. When they saw that he had lost consciousness, they threw him onto the boiling-hot bath-floor to see if he was still alive. He lay there without moving but it's unclear whether he had passed out or was pretending to have done so. Either way, they thought he was dead.

So they carried him out of the bathhouse as if they had found him after he had fainted as a result of the heat. Some of his more faithful slaves and his mistresses took over, and there was a great deal of crying and wailing because they thought he had died. But the effect of all this noise was that it brought him round, helped no doubt by the fact that he was now out of the bathhouse and in the fresh air. His eyes flickered and his limbs moved so everyone could clearly see that he was alive. At this, the slaves who had attacked him fled, as they realised that the truth of what they had done would come out. Most of them were arrested and Macedo himself was kept alive with great difficulty for a few days but then died. He did at least have the consolation that all the slaves who had been involved and captured were tortured and then executed.

So you can see from these examples how we masters are exposed to all kinds of danger. Treat your slaves brutally and these risks increase. But you should not assume that you will be able to sleep soundly and securely if you treat your slaves indulgently and gently. Not all masters who are killed by their slaves deserve their fate because of their cruelty. Many are simply the victims of slaves who are naturally wicked and capable of the most criminal acts.

Even if hostile slaves do not go so far as to kill you, they can still inflict great harm. During one of the wars against Hannibal, a number of terrorist atrocities were committed in the city of Rome itself by persons who were supporters of the Carthaginians. Arson attacks targeted the forum, nearby shops, the state prison and a number of private houses. The Temple of Vesta was saved only with difficulty, primarily through the efforts of thirteen slaves who happened to be nearby and fetched water and stamped out the flames. They were subsequently freed as a reward. The fire was fierce and because it had broken out in several places there was no doubt that it had been started intentionally. So the senate announced that anyone who provided information about the culprits would be rewarded with money if they were free, and liberty if they were slaves. As a result of this incentive, a slave called Manus, who belonged to a Campanian noble family, came forward and denounced his owners. The parents of this family had been beheaded by Quintus Fulvius, and the five sons, so the slave said, had started the fires as revenge and to help Hannibal. He also said they were planning many more such attacks.

The sons were arrested. At first they denied the story, claiming that the slave had run away the previous day after he had been whipped as a punishment, and he was simply acting out of desire for revenge. But when they were interrogated with their accomplices in the forum, they all confessed. They were all executed but Manus was given his freedom and almost ten thousand sesterces. Now obviously in this case we must delight in the fact that enemies of the Roman state were exposed by a brave slave. But you should realise that discontented slaves within the household have a great capacity to reveal information about you that can be at best embarrassing, at worst downright dangerous.

You must also realise that most of the ways in which your slaves will resist you is not in the style of Spartacus, whose bravery defied his servile status. There is a whole range of things they can do to try to gain some minor victory over you in everyday life. It is this kind of small-scale defiance that you will have to be alert to each and every day you own slaves. They will lie to you about how much food they have taken, or they will cheat you out of some small change by claiming that something costs ten sesterces when in fact it cost eight. They will pretend to be too ill to work and from the great groans and moans they emit you will think it a miracle if they survive, when in fact they are simply acting to get out of some difficult task. They will stand in the kitchen near the oven to generate heat and a sweat and then will stagger towards you as if collapsing from fever.

In the country your estate slaves will claim to have sown more seed than they have actually used. They will steal from your storage barns to supplement their rations; they will fiddle the books to show that the harvest is not quite as plentiful as you supposed and then sell the surplus in the local market. Or they will just take their time about everything, dawdling along as they work so that a job that should last for an hour or two takes a whole day. And when you complain they will swear by the gods that it was a much more difficult job than you realised and honestly they were doing their best. And if you are not careful you will believe their lies and before long every task that has to be carried out on the farm starts to take twice as long as it should. This is how slaves operate. They constantly push at the boundaries to see what they can get away with. And if you are not careful it will steadily chip away at your authority until it is entirely eaten up and your slaves treat you with disdain.

Lazy and sleepy city slaves will sneak off into town so they can hang around in bars, or watch the chariot-racing or gamble on the street corners. Or they will go to the baths and enjoy a good soak and a steam at your expense, then enjoy sitting about with their friends from other households, chatting or flirting with slave girls. And when you ask where they have been they will say how busy the streets were and what queues there were. Or they will just stare at you blankly and pretend they are too stupid to understand what you are talking about.

But a lot of slaves are nowhere near as dim-witted as they make out to be. You should read the story about that clever slave called Aesop, who was always outwitting his master. He does things like taking everything literally:

'Where were you born?' asked his master.

'In my mother's belly,' replies Aesop.

'No, in what place were you born?' tried the master again.

'My mother didn't tell me whether it was the bedroom or the dining room.'

You should remember the old proverb that 'a clever slave shares the power', meaning of course that if you do not stay on your guard you will end up having the household slaves deciding who does what when.

Or they act like complete cowards whenever any vaguely dangerous job comes up. Or they try to appeal to your softer side. It is one of the great irritations of owning slaves that they are constantly coming up to you in tears, begging you to forgive them this or let them off that. Naturally you should try to harden your heart but when it is domestic slaves who have provided good service it is sometimes difficult not to yield. But then you must be on the lookout for those domestic slaves who can kick like an ass. They will spit in your soup, or hide your books just to annoy you or, as even happened to me once, will pretend to trip and pour the fish sauce over your head. I can assure you that I was not fooled by that old trick. Running away is another way they can steal your property and getting them back is tedious and time-consuming. Even then, you are stuck with a recalcitrant slave who has no wish to please you.

You must always bear in mind that your typical slave is impudent, gossiping, lazy, deceitful, light-fingered and unscrupulous. Very few meet your expectations of a loyal, industrious, diligent and thrifty servant. Even fewer obey you with fear and trembling and in singleness of heart, as they should. Instead, the work-shy and untrustworthy majority spend their time trying to avoid your supervision. They will have parties at night while you sleep and you will wonder how it is that all your slave girls are suddenly getting pregnant.

They will gossip about you and if you treat them harshly they will go about behind your back telling stories about you to slaves in other households. They would rather reveal their master's secrets than steal his best Falernian wine. You will then find your friends asking you impertinent questions at dinner parties about your alleged vicious treatment of your slaves. It is all designed to get you to change your behaviour. They figure that you will not want to be thought of as a brutal and unjust master among your friends and acquaintances. Who, after all, can ever aspire to such a reputation?

So you must be careful to treat your household slaves with some consideration, especially if you are planning to run for political office, because damaging gossip often emanates from households. Otherwise, if you are careful with your management of household provisions you find stories going around about what a great miser you are. Indeed, when I stood for office I recall being advised that the most important thing to do is to remember people's names, even the slaves', for nothing is so popular or pleasing.

Of course no slave would ever say any of this to your face. They are too cowardly for that. If they do want to speak to you about some important matter you often find them using fables. Fables were actually invented to enable a slave to express feelings and thoughts that he otherwise would not dare say aloud for fear of punishment. So if they think you are doing something too quickly they will start telling you the story about the tortoise and the hare. It can be terribly annoying.

Gossip is an annoyance but plotting is dangerous. It is the clandestine meetings that take place in hushed tones that you need to be particularly careful to stamp out. Or ban them from using their own kind of language if they start doing that. For they will sometimes invent their own phrases and words that mean nothing to you but conceal their true intentions. There can only be one use for a private language of this kind: sedition.

A more harmless thing slaves do when they get together is tell each other silly tales in which they get the better of you, the master. In their imaginations, they outwit you and leave you looking foolish. I dare say it makes them feel better about their lowly status and their lack of power. Or they use them to give each other useful advice. One I overheard recently was a story about a jackdaw, which was kept as a pet on a piece of string. It tried to escape but the string got caught, and as he lay dying, the bird said, 'Stupid idiot! I couldn't bear being a slave but now I've robbed myself of life itself.' As the storyteller said, 'Servants long for their old masters only when they get a taste of new ones.' Which is true indeed.

Another malevolent act which the disgruntled slave

can carry out against you is to employ the black arts of magic. Naturally, I do not myself believe in the power of sorcery to hurt me, but most of the household does and if it gets around that you have had a spell put on you it can generate a general feeling of unease. Unfortunately it can be very hard to detect. For the slaves will often simply have their curse written on a lead tablet and place it among the tombs on the edge of town, the idea being that you the master will soon end up yourself as one of the corpses buried there.

This anonymous kind of resistance against you is common. It leaves a bad taste in the mouth that those whom you endeavour to treat fairly and justly go behind your back to express their discontent. But in reality it is harmless and they only do it anonymously because they fear you and what you will do to them if they are discovered. You must learn to take it as a compliment to your authority and to the disciplined way in which you manage your household.

·· COMMENTARY ··

Falx reveals the fears and anxieties that weighed on a master's mind in this chapter. The story of Spartacus is famous as a result of the 1960 Stanley Kubrick film starring Kirk Douglas. But the image of the heroic freedom fighter, inspiring his followers to stand up and claim collectively that 'I'm Spartacus!', gives a false picture of relations between masters and slaves in the Roman world. Given that Roman Italy was one of the great slave-owning societies in history, it is not surprising to find that slaves carried out many acts of resistance. A Roman proverb said that there were as many enemies as there were slaves – *quot servi tot hostes*. But such resistance did not always have to be as dramatic as that of Spartacus in 73–71 BC. In fact, slave rebellions were rare and, with the exception of Spartacus's revolt, easily crushed. These revolts were concentrated in periods when there had been a large influx of slaves into a relatively small geographical area. Often the slaves came from similar ethnic backgrounds, meaning that it was easier for them to discuss plans. It also helped that their previous military leadership was still present among their ranks. The huge supply of slaves after republican Rome's massive conquests made slaves cheap and expendable. There was no incentive for masters to treat their assets decently. This proved a dangerous combination of factors, but it was a mix that only rarely emerged.

By the time of the empire the slave system was too well oiled to face serious, large-scale threats. Slave resistance coalesced around small acts of lying, cheating, pretending to be ill, and going slow. Such small-scale defiance took many forms and was not always confrontational, involving passive tactics such as evasion and pretending to be stupid. We must be careful not to dramatise social relations into a model that sees Roman society as involved in a constant class conflict between owners and their human capital.

Characters like Bulla Felix can easily be read today as

Robin Hood figures: social bandits who turn the injustice of the normal world on its head and form an egalitarian community to resist the corruption of the regime. However these are texts written for an upper-class audience and it is more likely that the characters within them are a literary convention used to highlight the poor governance of certain corrupt officials and emperors. Nonetheless, the bandit stories do use popular themes of injustice, poverty and corruption to exert pressure on poor-quality rulers. Such stories threw the government's own standards back in its face when it fell short.

Some acts of slave resistance can be seen as negotiating techniques between slaves and their masters. By probing to see what they could get away with, they tried to chip away at the boundaries that enslaved them. Being a coward could be a useful tactic for a slave because it might prevent him from being placed in any position of danger. Another was to appeal to the master's soft side, if he had one. Seneca mentions that one of the irritations of owning slaves was that it meant relying on people who were always breaking down in tears (*On Tranquillity of the Mind* 8.8). Such crying could have been an actual expression of distress or it could have been a tactic to try to avoid an unpleasant task or punishment. Owners often denied the humanity of their slaves, seeing them as little more than animals. By breaking down in tears, the slaves could try to reverse this process and assert their humanity, showing masters the effects of their brutal treatment. This was probably a tactic that was only likely to benefit some domestic slaves, who were in a position to have some kind of direct relationship with their master.

Gossip was also a way for slaves to try to actively alter their master's behaviour. Gossip advertised a master's maltreatment to a wider audience. It suggested that the master was not a good man and reduced his standing in the community. Advice given to Cicero on electioneering warns that gossip often emanates from households. It says that even slaves should be treated with great consideration in the run-up to an election. Trickster tales, like those of the *Aesop Romance*, allowed the downtrodden to enjoy situations where the little man won, albeit temporarily. The trickster hero was a clever mischief-maker, who overturned the normal world where the master was in charge. Such a symbolic levelling provided a kind of psychic revenge against the rich, which was in itself a kind of empowerment. Whether any of this kind of small-scale or passive resistance ever really amounted to much is impossible to say.

The account of the First Slave War in Sicily of *c.*135–132 BC is in Diodorus Siculus 34.2. The accounts of Spartacus's rebellion are in Plutarch's *Life of Crassus* and Appian *Civil Wars* 1.14. The story of terrorist attacks in Rome in support of Hannibal is at Livy 26.27. The murder of Larcius Macedo is described in Pliny the Younger *Letters* 3.14. Bulla Felix is to be found in Dio Cassius 77.10.

CHAPTER IX

SETTING SLAVES FREE

MANY SLAVES LONG for freedom. Despite the fact that they have no social value they feel humiliated and degraded by their treatment. And even though they are, as a rule, morally worthless they think they deserve to be free. Many of them even seem to feel that it is somehow unjust that they are slaves, even in cases when the moral and legal arguments against them are watertight.

That slaves know they may be freed is actually of great benefit to the owner. It is a carrot with which to incentivise the slave to work diligently and honestly. It is also a stick with which to punish him if he disappoints you in some way. Hope can help men endure all kinds of suffering. Hopelessness can cause them to take desperate measures.

In fact not all slaves want to be freed. Some are so contented within their household, enjoying a close relationship with their master, that there seems to be little to be gained by becoming free and taking on all the cares and responsibilities of that status. There is the famous case of Gaius Melissus, who was born free at Spoleto, but abandoned as a baby because his parents could not agree what to do with him. A local man rescued him and brought him up as a slave, but educated him to a high standard. Eventually he presented the slave as a gift to the emperor Augustus's close friend Maecenas to use as a letter-writer. Melissus soon realised that Maecenas treated him as an equal on account of his fine intellect, even accepting him as he would a friend. At this point, his mother suddenly appeared and tried to claim back his freedom, hoping no doubt to get some financial advantage from having a son who was close to the centre of power. But Melissus decided that he would prefer to remain as a slave, since, as Maecenas's friend, his status could not be improved. Maecenas soon afterwards set him free anyway because of these noble sentiments and Melissus even became friendly with Augustus himself. Indeed the emperor appointed him to build up the library in the Portico of Octavia.

Bequeathing freedom in a will is the most common form of setting slaves free. But if you choose to do it while you are still alive there is the ancient rod ceremony. In this, you as the master appear before a magistrate who publicly affirms the slave's new freedom. You then give the slave a slap as a final insult for them to suffer at your hands. There are also more informal methods should you not want to go through such a ritual. The old-fashioned way is to hold the slave's hand, say, 'I want this man to be free,' and then let go of him. This is where we get our word for freeing slaves from, to 'manumit', meaning literally to let him go from your hand.

Often I have simply written a letter to the slave, or I have invited him to sit at table and join me and my friends for dinner, thereby announcing it to them as witnesses. I rather like such relaxed arrangements within the household. The best slaves are those who become part of the family and so it is nice to carry out the procedure among other members of the household. I like it best if I can surprise them – it is a delight to see the mix of shock, joy and gratitude on their faces. The only disadvantage with this is that the rod ceremony is required for the slave to get full legal citizenship, but this can always be done at a later date as a formality.

Sadly, such acts of manumission are not free. The government taxes them at 5 per cent of the value of the slave. So many slaves are set free that it is a good source of revenue. As an owner you also have to be aware of the limits to manumission that were laid down by Augustus. The emperor was concerned that mass manumission would dilute the strong citizen body of Romans with too many weaklings and foreigners. He therefore decreed that only a certain maximum percentage of a master's slaves could be set free in a will. The percentage varied according to how many slaves the master owned. A master who owned between two and ten slaves, which is probably by far the most common number, could manumit half of them; if he had between ten and thirty he could free a third, but only a quarter if he possessed between thirty and a hundred. The largest owners, with between one hundred and five hundred slaves, could release only one-fifth of them. Augustus also imposed a variety of other conditions designed to prevent the worst kind of slaves from becoming citizens. So slaves who had ever been tortured or branded were banned from becoming citizens no matter how they had been manumitted.

When to free is a difficult decision. The main distinction to draw is whether you are setting the slave free because of emotional bonds you have developed with him or because he has paid you money. When it comes to faithful domestic slaves who have given you years of loyal service, then my view, one shared with most others I know, is that it is right and proper for them to be rewarded with their freedom. I once freed a highly intelligent secretary of mine called Tiro, because he had always proved completely trustworthy and diligent, and he was such a civilised character that his former condition was below his real station in life. I preferred to have him as a friend than as a slave, a view that my whole family shared. My wife jumped for joy at the decision. That reminds me that I haven't heard back from him yet. I heard he was ill and wrote to him more than once but he hasn't replied. These freedmen! He deserves a good beating!

Many a master has released a female slave because he has grown affectionate towards her, and wants that relationship to become a legitimate marriage. While this is perhaps reprehensible in some ways, it is hardly surprising that a master who is single sometimes grows close to an attractive young slave girl who is eager to please him. If you find yourself in that position make sure that you release the girl on condition of marriage. I know of several old fools who have fallen for a slave girl, released them in the expectation of marriage, only for them to run off with some younger man. Or it is frequently the case that some freedman of yours will offer to pay you to release a slave you still own, with whom he had been having a relationship when he was still a slave. On such occasions it seems churlish to deny a loyal servant his opportunity for marital bliss. It once even happened that a freedwoman of mine came back to buy her man from me. Again, I could hardly say no given her long years of loyal service and the fact that she had delivered me three healthy sons.

With slave women I would not normally consider freeing them until they are past childbearing age or have been productive in this regard. The household has too great a need for home-bred slaves to permit such an indulgence on the part of the master.

What length of service deserves to be rewarded with liberty? There is an argument for setting a maximum limit on the number of years' service required to achieve manumission. A total of twenty or thirty years of servitude seems too harsh for anyone to bear. I generally feel that thirty is a good age at which to free a slave, giving them time to establish themselves in society and continue to deliver you good service as a loyal freedman. There are some who feel that only five or six years of servitude are enough. If a Roman soldier fell into slavery as the result of being captured in war and had to be ransomed by the state, he paid back the cost of his ransom with five years' service as a slave of the state. In the republic, the orator Cicero said that the first six years of Julius Caesar's dictatorship was equivalent to a full term of slavery for the Roman people.

Some special situations call for flexibility. Recently, for example, I was very distressed by an outbreak of severe illness among my household, which resulted in the deaths of two younger slaves. I am always ready to grant my slaves their freedom in such circumstances on their deathbed, so that they and those close to them can find some solace in the fact that they are dying free men. I do, however, normally make a provision for recovery so that they cannot feign sickness or simply walk away if they miraculously get better. I might also add here that I usually allow my household slaves to make their own wills and to bequeath their wealth and possessions as they wish. Even though slaves cannot make wills, I treat these as legally binding, as if they were real, so long as they keep their bequests within the household. It is actually my money, after all.

For your information, it is perhaps worth knowing that slaves who belong to the state can also be manumitted. Sometimes this takes place when the slave manages to buy a replacement for his own job. This can create legal problems. I remember that a slave belonging to our town council bought his freedom by providing a replacement slave who then ran away. The council tried to make him submit again to the yoke of slavery but he wrote to the emperor who said that his manumission was legal and there was no provision for him to return if his replacement ran away, so he remained a free man.

Very occasionally the state will set slaves free so that they can serve in the army, since only those freeborn can fight as soldiers. As you can imagine, it is only in the direst circumstances that this has happened, such as after the great defeat suffered by our forces at Cannae at the hands of Hannibal or when Varus lost three legions in the Teutoburg forest during the time of Augustus.

There are many bad reasons for freeing your slaves. Freedom should be the reward for loyal service, not just granted at the whim of the master. Regrettably, there have been a number of cases where slaves have been freed for helping their masters carry out crimes and even murders. Or they have been freed so that as citizens they can receive the monthly corn dole and handouts from the government. That way they will be fed at the state's expense and not their master's. Others have been freed for the silliest of reasons. I personally know people who granted freedom to as many slaves as possible after their own deaths, so that they could have an impressive funeral. They have been carried to their tombs accompanied by a great cortège of freedmen wearing their felt liberty-caps, even though some of them were slaves of the worst kind. Most true Romans have not been impressed when they have seen these processions, rather they have been horrified at how these dregs of humanity are now becoming citizens.

You should also be aware that you cannot simply dump your slaves when you have finished with them, as Cato advises. Back in the days of the emperor Claudius, some owners were abandoning their sick or old slaves on the Tiber island where there is a temple to the god of health, Asclepius. The emperor decreed that any slave abandoned in this way was to be set free, and would not have to go back to their master if they recovered, since a slave's obligations to his master stopped if the master forgot his obligations to the slave. Claudius also stated that any master who killed a slave rather than abandon him would be prosecuted for murder. He enacted these laws not so much because he was concerned about the humane treatment of slaves, but because the law had become unclear regarding such situations and it seemed right that the emperor should clarify the position for all.

The other main reason for freeing a slave is that he has bought his freedom from you. Selling slaves their freedom is a great benefit to us owners. This might at first sight seem counter-intuitive since the effect is for us to lose slaves rather than retain them. But you should remember that your body of slaves is a constantly evolving organism. Old blood will be replaced by new, which will help keep your slaves as a whole fresh and hard-working. So if you can charge your slave for his freedom so much the better, for he is then giving you the capital with which to replace him. It need cost you nothing.

The owner can in this way make the most of servile aspirations for freedom. Slaves have their own money and possessions, even though these are legally yours. They acquire possessions because it is usual to pay them something in return for good work. This is a good investment because you will get it all back. For you will find that slaves will pay handsomely to secure their freedom, even if it is at some uncertain future date, such as their master's death.

You should also be aware of some of the pitfalls here. So great is many slaves' desire for liberty that they will make huge sacrifices to acquire it. It is common practice to give domestic, urban slaves a little money to buy their own food. Often, they will save up to buy their freedom by robbing their stomachs. If you are not careful you can find that your personal attendants look like a collection of skeletons.

These agreements between master and slave are legally enforceable. So if any slave claims to have bought himself free with his own money, but that his master has reneged on the deal, then he can lodge a complaint before the urban prefect. If the slave cannot prove it then he will be sent to work in the mines as a punishment for wasting everyone's time and tarnishing the reputation of his master. Alternatively, the master can ask for the slave to be returned to him so that he can inflict his own punishment upon him, so long as it is not more severe than being sent to the mines.

Given that these arrangements are legally binding, it is important to have a contract drawn up to formalise matters. When I do this with one of my domestic slaves, the contract is then lodged at the nearby temple for safekeeping.

Setting a slave free in this way does not always mean he is immediately free to do as he pleases. Generally I will stipulate a number of conditions before the act of manumission finally takes place. Firstly, I demand a term of further service, usually for a number of years. During this period he remains a slave in practice, even if he is nominally freed and under the ownership of the temple's god. The slave in question must promise to give good service and to do as he is told. He has to confirm that he will continue to submit to physical punishment from me, in whatever form I decide upon. If the slave is a woman I often stipulate that she must hand over one of her children as a replacement. They are normally happy to do this, since they want their freedom, have children to spare, hope to buy the child's freedom at some point in the future, and the child is in any case perfectly used to his situation in my household. Sometimes, if I am particularly reluctant to lose the slave because they perform some valuable service to me, I set the period of further service for as long as I shall live.

I have also stipulated in my will that certain other slaves will be freed. I have, however, placed conditions upon this, namely that they will continue to provide my widow with particular services. In some instances I have linked certain of my slaves' freedom in my will to the payment of instalments to my son and heir over a period of between three and five years. In this way, my son will receive the benefit of both an income and a period of continued labour. I have also placed certain demands on my son that he continues to look after two of my old retainers even when I am deceased. This is an indulgence on my part and a small burden on him, but it will enable my spirit to rest more easily.

I cannot emphasise enough how important it is to make sure the contracts are watertight. I know of one friend, now dead, who, during an illness, was in his haste to leave a will and misspelt his favourite slave's name, thereby decreeing that he was freeing Cratinus when the slave's actual name was Cratistus. The matter went to court in the end, where it was, thankfully, decided that the slave should be freed, on the principle that freedom should be favoured wherever possible.

Once freed, your freedmen continue to have a close relationship to you. You are now their patron, as you were once their master. And where they used to have to give unswerving obedience as slaves, they are now expected to show you deference and the kind of obedience that a son should show to his father. For the figure of father and patron ought always to be respected and sacred in the eyes of a freedman or a son. Even if they move out, they are still part of your household.

When they are freed I make them swear an oath that they will continue to work for me for free for a specified number of days each year. As such, they are expected to help you when required and perform various small services. This can take whatever form is appropriate to their trade: the painting of a room if they are painters, cutting hair if they are barbers, and so on. This can even be required of children who have had their freedom bought by their parents. For children can still be useful to you in a variety of ways, such as someone who calls out guests' names as they arrive or as some kind of entertainer. Of course, you cannot be too demanding of your freedmen when it comes to this work. You are not allowed to ask them to do things that they are unable to do, either through lack of strength or skill. And you cannot force the freedman to work so much that he is unable to earn his living on the other days. If you do this you will find that he will take you to court and you will lose.

Freedmen are particularly useful as agents to pursue your interests. I have set up numbers of my freedmen in business, as bankers and moneylenders, but also in overseas trade. All of these activities are highly profitable but are too vulgar for a man of high social standing to become involved with directly.

In return for these services, the freedmen gets patronage from you. This can be in the form of financial assistance, for example setting them up in business, providing contacts, and helping to open up doors. Often I am asked to write letters of reference for my freedmen, an act which I am always happy to do if they have proved worthy of it. Their status as dependants of my household should also ensure that I continue to provide something for them in their old age. And, once dead, as members of my household they are allowed to share the Falx family tomb, although I retain the right to exclude those whom I do not deem worthy of such an honour. I also make sure that a key to the tomb is available to their families so that they can carry out as many sacrifices as they care to.

Some masters grow particularly attached to their slaves and acts of extreme generosity have been recorded. I know of one old family servant who was pensioned off with a small estate. She had been the family nurse and had been almost a mother to the master's children. So when the son inherited, and the nurse was too old to be of further service, he gave her a farm worth 100,000 sesterces. I have to say, though, that such acts are rare.

On the whole, you will find your freedmen a pleasant and grateful bunch. I have been mentioned on the tombs of many of my freedmen who have since passed away. One recent one reads as follows: 'To my most well-deserving patron, Marcus Sidonius Falx, I give thanks in return for his many kindnesses.' Charm and virtue combined. We should not be surprised that our freedmen are grateful to us. We have bought them as worthless slaves, captured from some barbarian tribe, or if they are home-breds we have brought them up at our own expense. Then, after due service, we have given them an opportunity to find their way in the greatest society the world has ever known. As full citizens, they and their descendants can hold their heads up high among the most successful and civilised citizens on earth.

The household offers them a home and a hearth, a base on which to build their lives. Many of my slaves become great friends with each other, a friendship that lasts into liberty. Two of my freedmen first met on the slave-dealer's platform, learnt Latin together, and then set up in business together once they had been freed. When one died, the other paid for an expensive tombstone to his 'dearest companion'. It is different in the country estate where only the bailiffs usually have the money to set up such tombstones. Even then most of them do not do so, not because they cannot read or write, but because there is no one else to read them. I have myself, at my own expense, set up a tombstone for one most faithful and efficient farm manager I owned. The field slaves do not generally have the time or money to spend thinking about funeral monuments.

Being a slave is a terrible fate, but in Rome it need not be the end. I urge slaves to see it as a test, which, if they pass and prove themselves to be good, loyal and trustworthy, can provide a route to becoming a genuine Roman.

·· COMMENTARY ··

For many Roman slaves, servitude was a temporary situation. If they worked hard and honestly and served their master well they could reasonably expect to be granted their freedom. What is impossible to know is what percentage of slaves this reasonable expectation might have applied to. It is also unclear how long slaves would have had to have waited for their freedom. It seems clear that domestic slaves were more likely to be manumitted because some of them were in a position to develop a personal relationship with their master. Not all domestic slaves, particularly in the larger households, would have been in a position to do this, as the master would have remained a distant and aloof figure.

Manumission was primarily an urban phenomenon. There are examples of bailiffs being freed in the country but it seems more likely that field labourers were generally worked until they dropped. It is not hard to see why this was the case. The master had minimal contact with them, would benefit little from any services they would subsequently provide as freedmen, and would then have to replace them. Perhaps the best that could be hoped for is that the older farm slaves were allocated to the gentler tasks instead of the back-breaking toil in the fields. Not many are likely to have lived into old age in any case.

The length of servitude that a domestic slave might expect to serve seems to have varied greatly. The few comments that survive suggest anything from five or six years to closer to twenty. One interesting perspective on this question is provided by the *Oracles of Astrampsychus*. One of the questions comes clearly from the mouth of a slave: 'Will I be freed from servitude?' The answers suggest that for most slaves freedom was constantly pushed off into the distance. Of the ten possible answers, five say 'not yet', two say 'after some time', and another 'once you've paid', which could be any time but is likely to be some time off given that the slave had to save a lot of money to do this. One gives an outright 'no' and advises the slave to 'be silent'. Only one is optimistic: he will be freed 'with a good bequest'. This was the life that many slaves lived, one of permanently hoping for a better future And from the master's point of view it made sense to keep the slaves hanging on for as long as possible to maximise the return from the asset, while the prospect of freedom kept the slave working diligently and honestly.

The details stipulated in the Delphi manumission contracts show that even when such freedom was attained it was often put off for years and was conditional upon continued good service. The various duties which the freedman was often expected to continue to carry out for his former master also show that the divide between slavery and freedom was not, in practice, as clear-cut as we might imagine. That said, it is obvious that many slaves longed to be free and were prepared to go to great lengths to achieve it.

Slavery was a way for Roman society to assimilate large numbers of outsiders into its structure. But the Romans did try to erect some kind of quality control to prevent undesirables from becoming citizens. The *Lex*

Aelia Sentia, for example, prevented any slaves from being freed who had been put in chains as a punishment by their masters or had been branded, or interrogated under torture about a crime they had committed, or had been sentenced to fight as gladiators or against wild beasts. Instead, if their owner manumitted them, they became free men of the same status as subject foreigners. The *Lex Fufia Caninia* of 2 BC set additional restrictions on the percentage of his slaves that a master could manumit (see Gaius *Institutes* 1, 1; 8–55; Suetonius *Augustus* 40).

Cicero's comment that the first six years of Julius Caesar's dictatorship was equivalent to a full term of slavery can be found at *Philippic* 8.11.32. One of Augustus's most severe punishments was to forbid slaves from being freed for thirty years (Suetonius *Augustus* 21). *Digest* 38.1 deals with the laws regarding the work obligations of freedmen to their patrons. Claudius bans owners from abandoning sick or old slaves on the Tiber island in Suetonius *Claudius* 25. On masters freeing their slaves so that they would receive the state corn dole, see the *Theodosian Code* 14.17.6 and Suetonius *Augustus* 42. For the gift of a farm to the old nurse, see Pliny the Younger *Letters* 6.3. The inscription *ILS* 8365 is an example of a tomb being open to the wider members of the household, including slaves and freedmen. The tale of Gaius Melissus is at Suetonius *Grammarians* 5.

· CHAPTER X ·

THE PROBLEM WITH FREEDMEN

A MBITION IS THE INTELLECTUAL equivalent
of body odour. This is the problem with freedmen – they reek of it. Once they have formally been
welcomed as Roman citizens, they feel a desperate urge
to climb socially. It is not wholly surprising if freedmen
who were branded or tattooed as slaves should try to
conceal these physical reminders of their servitude by
visiting doctors who specialise in concealing the marks
by digging them out and burning the flesh so it scars
over. But most freedmen go much further. They strive
hard for success, far harder, it has to be admitted, than
most of the freeborn would care to. It is a blessing that
they are prohibited from holding office, for otherwise
they would all be frantically clambering up the greasy
pole of the political career. So instead, they are forced
to fulfil their desire for personal achievement by means
of getting rich. But even this they can achieve only in a
vulgar manner. For instead of drawing an income from
the long-term custody and management of landholdings,

they often try to make their wealth by trade. As a result, they are proverbially rich.

Freeing slaves is always an indulgence. The master, looking back fondly to the many years of honest service which a particular slave has given, will soften and seek to feel that warm glow of approbation which the act of manumission engenders. Like him, we might think that our freedmen would be overcome with gratitude towards us; that they would be keen to reimburse us for our generosity and kindliness; or that there would be nothing they would not do to help us in some small way. We might care to imagine that the slave, once freed, will gladly act with due respect to his master's superior social position. We would be sadly wrong. For freedmen often do not act as obsequiously as they should. Instead they often have many upstart ideas well above their station, however much it has been improved.

As an example, I give you my freedman Servius. I rewarded him, an educated man, with his freedom and, as is usual practice, he took my name: Marcus Sidonius Servius. Yet no sooner had he been freed from his bonds than he felt able to behave towards me as if he were some kind of equal. He addressed me with familiarity and rarely bothered to turn up to pay his respects in the morning. On one occasion, he even took to interrupting me as I was explaining to him what I wanted him to do with his business venture, for which I was providing financial backing. My temper snapped. I administered a light beating of a few slaps and told him in no uncertain terms what I thought of his behaviour. You will not believe what happened next. He took me to court. The cheek of it! He argued that I had dishonoured him as a free man by treating him in this way. Naturally the judge, who is a man whom I have for many years known to possess sound judgement, did not see the matter in the same way. He dismissed the case, saying that it was absurd for a piece of former property to claim dishonour from his former owner. As a former slave, he could never have any honour in the eyes of his former master, so it was impossible to dishonour him.

Sadly, not all freedmen are grateful to you, nor do they all carry out their duties as they should. On several occasions I myself have been forced to go to court to complain about certain of my freedmen. The courts, rightly, condemn such behaviour by freedmen: former slaves cannot be allowed to get away with it. If they behave insolently or abusively, they are generally punished, perhaps even with a period of exile. Or if they have attacked their patron, they will be condemned to hard labour in the mines. The same punishment will happen if they are found guilty of having spread malicious rumours about their patron or incited someone to bring an accusation against him. If they have merely failed to carry out their work duties for their former master, they will usually receive a telling-off only, but be warned that they will be severely punished if they give cause for complaint again. The emperor Claudius went so far as to sell back into slavery any freedman who failed to show due gratitude to their patrons or about whom their former owners had cause for complaint.

The burning ambition that drives these freedmen and their families has seen some rise in society to an almost phenomenal extent. It does seem scandalous that an ex-slave can, through work or inheritance of their former master's estate, equal the wealth of the most established landowning families. I have the dubious pleasure of having one of them as a neighbour in Campania, where the fellow has bought a typically ostentatious and over-priced estate. His name is Trimalchio and he invited me over to dinner soon after arriving and, not wishing to seem aloof, I accepted. He spent the entire evening going on and on about how he had earnt it all by his own hard work. 'I've got drive,' he said. 'I buy low and I know when to sell high, and I am extremely mean and thrifty.'

He had come as a slave to Rome from Asia as a boy and was used by his master as his favourite for fourteen years. Eventually he managed the whole household and was named as heir by his master, from whom he inherited in due course. As he said, 'no one is satisfied with doing nothing', so he decided to go into business. He built five ships and filled them with wine, but they all sank on the way to Rome. He claims to have lost 30 million sesterces but that kind of gross exaggeration is typical of his sort. So he built bigger and better ships and loaded them with wine, bacon, beans, perfumes and slaves. On one voyage he says he made a profit of 10 million sesterces – believe him if you will – and then acquired himself a huge house, many slaves and an estate.

It does seem outrageous that these nouveau riche are so visibly successful. You would think that they would just be glad to be free and be quietly grateful to the citizen body that has accepted them into its heart. As it is, the Roman people have become a melting pot for all kinds of immigrants and ex-slaves. Sometimes even the vast difference in status between the free and slaves is ignored. Since the emperor Augustus reformed the Order of the Knights to admit those worth over 400,000 sesterces, it has become jammed full of wealthy freedmen. Boundaries are becoming so blurred that freedmen are even managing to get themselves elected to high office. Barbarius Philippus, for example, was a runaway slave but was illegally elected as praetor at Rome. It makes one wonder whether all his decrees should be wiped off the statutes or whether they should remain for the sake of stability.

Certainly when freedmen and slaves are discovered trying to lie and cheat their way into public office, then they should be punished vigorously. One slave called Maximus was about to enter the office of quaestor when his owner recognised him and dragged him away. He was actually granted immunity because he had dared to stand for public office, but another runaway who was found to have become one of the praetors already was thrown from the Tarpeian Rock on the Capitol. Nowadays, things are in such chaos and confusion and the fine traditions of the Roman state are so widely ignored that, as far as I can see, slaves buy their freedom and become Romans with money they have got through robbery, prostitution and other nefarious activities.

I know that some local communities take great exception when a wealthy former slave starts upsetting the apple cart. I remember that this happened near my estate in Africa, when a newly freed slave called Chresimus started getting much bigger harvests from his small farm than did his neighbours with far larger holdings. He became extremely unpopular and people accused him of stealing their crops through sorcery. During his trial he brought all his farm equipment into the forum along with his slaves. His tools were well fashioned and kept, while his slaves were all healthy, well dressed and well looked after. 'Here is my magic,' he shouted. 'But the invisible ingredient is my work and the sweat I've poured early in the morning till late at night.' They acquitted him unanimously.

To be fair, there are many freedmen and their sons who have made a huge commercial success out of farming. Acilius Sthenelus, who was the son of a freed-man, won great honour by cultivating no more than sixty acres of vines in the territory of Nomentum and selling it for 400,000 sesterces. Sthenelus also aided his friend Remmius Palaemon, who within the past two decades bought for 600,000 sesterces a country estate in the same territory of Nomentum, about ten miles outside Rome. As you may know, the price of all suburban property is notoriously low, particularly in this region, but he even bought the cheapest farms, which had been ruined by neglect and whose soil was poor even by the worst standards. Under Sthenelus's careful management the vineyards were replanted, the soil improved and farm buildings rebuilt. The result was extraordinary: within eight years the unharvested vintage was auctioned to a buyer for 400,000 sesterces. In the end the great philosopher and politician Seneca bought the vineyards for four times the original price, after just ten years of careful cultivation.

And we must also accept that not all freedmen are vulgar. Some have brains of the highest order and have contributed greatly to scholastic studies. This is not simply from being used by their literary-minded masters as readers or secretaries. Marcus Antonius Gnipho, for example, was born in Gaul of free birth, but was abandoned by his parents and raised as a slave. The man who reared him first educated him and then freed him. He is said to have been extremely talented, with an unparalleled memory, learned in both Greek and Latin, and had a pleasant and easy-going manner. He never asked to be paid for his teaching but, instead, relied on the generosity of his pupils. He even taught in the household where Julius Caesar grew up. Or there was Staberius Eros, probably a Thracian, who was bought at a public auction but later freed because of his love of literature. He loved the republic. He taught Caesar's assassins, Brutus and Cassius. And he was endowed with such a noble character that, during Sulla's dictatorship, he taught the children of those who had fallen foul of the tyrant for free. And then there was Lenaeus, who was the freedman of Pompey the Great and went with him everywhere, even on most of his expeditions. The story goes that when he was still a slave he escaped from his chains and fled back to his own country, where he taught literature. He then sent his master the same amount of money that he had paid for him, but his master set him free for nothing since he had such an excellent character and was such a fine scholar.

The freedmen of the divine emperor's household are also, naturally, to be excepted from the characterisation of former slaves as vulgar parvenus. Their proximity to the father of the state gives them a special position in society. As slaves, they are paid by the emperor, and they often amass great fortunes and become slave owners themselves. Musicus Scurranus, for example, was an imperial slave of Tiberius who owned sixteen slaves himself. They performed a variety of services for him, and ranged from an accountant to a cook to a valet. Indeed, the uniqueness of such imperial freedmen was legally recognised under the emperor Claudius, who allowed them to marry citizens, and gave their children the status of Latins. Normal slaves, of course, would have been seriously punished if they had lived with a Roman citizen, and any children they produced would have been classed as slaves. And there are a great many of these imperial freedmen, who carry out a whole host of duties within the great imperial household. I even met one who had been the special keeper of the robes worn by the emperor at triumphs.

Some of these freedmen are so close to the emperor that they become their special confidants. Claudius, it is well known, looked to his freedmen for all kinds of advice, even in matters of public importance. He argued that since they could not stand for office themselves or be actively involved in political life, these freedmen could be relied upon to be entirely objective. There were even some freeborn citizens who voluntarily became slaves of the emperor to join his household and help him administer the empire. I know many of the older families were outraged that the jobs which had traditionally been carried out by senators were now being given to slaves. And it has to be said that some of them acted disgracefully. One of Claudius's freedmen, Pallas, was awarded

15 million sesterces and an honorary praetorship by the senate just for suggesting the legislation concerning imperial slaves being allowed to marry Roman women. In a carefully choreographed act of false modesty he turned the money down but took the honour, claiming that he would make do with his modest income. So the senate found itself in the absurd position of having to put up a public inscription praising the old-fashioned frugality of an ex-slave who was now worth some 300 million sesterces. At the same time, Pallas's brother, who was called Felix, did not show any such self-restraint. He had been appointed as governor of Judaea by Claudius and, believing himself safe because of his close relationship with the emperor, carried out all manner of crimes and confiscations in the province with impunity.

These imperial slaves and freedmen are a law unto themselves. They stand apart from the rest of society and this is seen most clearly in the close connections that they form with one another. I have seen several elaborate tombstones set up by one of them for a colleague who worked in the same part of the imperial administration. I have even seen tombs where they have chosen to lie together for eternity in death, so close was their relationship in life.

But these few exceptions aside, most freedmen cannot help but turn to ostentatious display to try to show that they are, in some sense, true Romans. You see it everywhere in their tombs. They seem to see this as their claim to some part of the eternal city and its citizen body. This is understandable enough but their tombs are always so grand and overly ornate and covered with self-aggrandising claims about the often very modest achievements of their occupants. Freedmen frequently assail you with details of how rich they are, failing to understand that true wealth does not need to advertise itself, for it speaks in the restrained manners and character of the gentleman. That neighbour of mine, Trimalchio, whom I mentioned before, bombarded me with details about how much wheat his estates produced and how many oxen had been broken that morning. He even had an accountant slave come in and recite details of what had been going on that day, announcing that thirty slaves boys had been born to Trimalchio's slave women, that a slave called Mithridates had been punished for cursing the master's name, that 10 million sesterces had been deposited in the strongboxes, and that there had been a fire in the gardens in Pompeii. Trimalchio broke in here:

'What was that,' he said, 'when did I buy gardens in Pompeii?'

'Last year,' the accountant replied, 'but they have yet to appear in the accounts.'

Trimalchio grew red with anger and proclaimed grandly:

'I forbid any estates that have been bought for me to be entered in my accounts if I have not been told about it within six months.'

All of this was the most embarrassing attempt to impress me and, naturally, I did not believe a word of any of it.

This all happened before the meal really got going. As we reclined for dinner, Egyptian slave boys ran up to us and poured water cooled with snow upon our hands, while others, who followed them in, clipped our toenails through the ends of our sandals with amazing dexterity. And while they were doing all these tasks, the boys sang aloud in harmony. The whole household seemed to be singing. Even when I ordered a drink from a boy nearby, he sang my order back to me in full cry. You would have imagined that you had not gone to dinner but to a concert in a theatre. Then the food started. A huge tray was brought in. On the tray stood a bronze donkey, on which hung two baskets carrying black and white olives respectively. Two platters contained an assortment of delicacies, including dormice sprinkled with poppy-seed and honey, and hot sausages on a silver gridiron, underneath which were damson plums and pomegranate seeds. The tray was engraved with Trimalchio's name and the weight of silver it contained.

We were in the middle of all these starters when Trimalchio himself was carried in, to the accompaniment of music. He was then placed on a pile of small cushions. His shaved head stuck out from a scarlet cloak and he had a napkin with a broad purple stripe, as if he were a senator, tucked around his neck. On the little finger of his left hand he wore a massive gold ring, and on the next finger, a slightly smaller one into which iron stars had been soldered. And then, in case all of this finery would not be visible, he bared his right arm, which was adorned with a golden armband and an ivory circlet clasped with a plate of shining gold.

The worst thing of all about this gaudy display was how proud he was of it. When Trimalchio caught sight of me smirking slightly at the excesses of his dinner, he was clearly very annoyed.

'What are you laughing at?' he said. 'You might be a Roman gentleman but I can walk among free men with my head held up high. I don't owe anyone a penny. I've never been taken to court and I've got no debts. Now I've bought some property and some silverware and have a household that has twenty slaves and a dog. I've been made a member of the College of the Six Priests of Augustus. I've even bought the slave woman I used to live with so that no one else can get their grubby hands on her.'

'Quite,' said I.

But he was in full flow now and was not to be stopped.

'You don't know what it was like to be a slave. What I hated was when you stuck-up Romans called me over shouting "boy, boy", especially when it was some teenager who hadn't grown a beard yet. Or when you're expected to bring them their chamber pot. Or when you're starving and you have to look at half-eaten cream cakes and chicken lying uneaten on the table but are told that it isn't right for a slave to eat any of these leftovers. But what made me really angry was when fat Romans called us slaves greedy gluttons, when we didn't get to eat any of these things. You know as well as I do, Falx, that all Romans just buy slaves to show off – it's not just us freedmen. We all buy as many as we can, not because they make us money but because they show people how rich and important we are.'

·· COMMENTARY ··

Freed slaves did not leave their former masters for a life of pure freedom. They were expected to display deference to the man who was now known as their patron, and, as his clients, they were obliged to carry out certain services for his benefit. The provision of such services could be enforced through the courts if the client failed to deliver them. Legally the master could no longer punish the slave physically but there is one example of a judge throwing out a complaint from a freedman who had suffered such an indignity at the hands of his patron. Cicero's letters to his intelligent former slave, Tiro, contain a number of joking references to how he will have to give him a good beating for failing to reply to his letters. It seems that masters continued to use a certain way of speaking to their freedmen, which they no doubt thought was hilarious but we can imagine was less so for those on the receiving end of it. See Mary Beard's article 'Ciceronian Correspondences: Making a Book out of Letters', In T. P. Wiseman (ed.), *Classics in Progress: Essays on Ancient Greece and Rome*, pp. 103–44.

Once freed from servitude, many former slaves worked hard to achieve what they had been unable to as slaves. Their pride at their achievements is best seen in the many tombstones that survive showing them in their togas, which they could wear only once they had become citizens. Numbers of them attained extraordinary wealth and power. Of course, these lucky few represent only the tip of the iceberg. But there were also countless more who managed to inch their way up the social ladder and improve their quality of life and that of their families to some small degree.

It was this kind of social mobility that distinguished Roman from Athenian slavery, where the citizen body was more fixed and less porous. By manumitting large numbers of slaves, Roman society was able to assimilate many new citizens. But that does not mean that their social success did not cause resentment. One document that is full of mockery for what it sees as these social upstarts is Petronius's *Satyricon*. Written in the mid-first century AD, the novel describes the misadventures of a man called Encolpius and his sixteen-year-old boyfriend, Giton. A long section of the work deals with a dinner they attend at the house of a fabulously wealthy freedman called Trimalchio. The meal is a catalogue of over-the-top extravagance and vulgarity, with the freedman making every effort to impress his guests through sheer ostentation. The text maintains a mocking sneer at such behaviour as well as ridiculing the lower-class speech and attitudes of Trimalchio and his circle of freedmen friends. But the *Satyricon* is a work of fiction; everything is deliberately exaggerated in order to make it funnier. Yet it is probably fair to see in it a reflection, albeit in grossly embellished form, of the resentment that high Roman society had towards those who managed to move up its social hierarchy.

Not all freedmen were the same, just as not all slaves were. Some had positions of great influence, such as those in the imperial household. Their proximity to the centre of power meant that they were treated as a special case in law. Others were gifted scholars and writers who achieved literary success. Most were nowhere near as successful as Trimalchio. Nor should we assume that there was a natural hostility between freedmen and their former masters. Many mention their gratitude towards their former owners for helping them in their later careers. Or they took advantage of the privilege to be buried in the tombs of their patron's family.

The legal rights of patrons can be found in *Digest* 37.14. On the different legal treatment of imperial freedmen see the *Theodosian Code* 4.12. The story of Acilius Sthenelus is in Pliny the Elder *Natural History* 14.5. For the accusations of magic against Furius Chresimus see Pliny the Elder *Natural History* 18.8.41–3. The slave Maximus who became quaestor is in Dio Cassius 48.34, and the slave Barbarius Philippus who was illegally elected as praetor at Rome is mentioned in *Digest* 1.14.3. The feast of Trimalchio is to be found in Petronius *Satyricon* 26–78.

· CHAPTER XI ·

CHRISTIANS AND
THEIR SLAVES

I T IS AN UNFORTUNATE FACT of the world we
now live in that there is an ever-growing number of
Christians. This wicked superstition was once held in
check by the vigorous actions of emperors such as Nero,
who killed many of them for their hatred of humanity.
But the evil again broke out in Judaea and soon found its
way back to Rome, where all things hideous and shame-
ful seem to find a home and become popular. I felt I
should add some final comments upon this strange sect
in case any of you barbarian readers have been so foolish
as to fall under its thrall.

It is a superstition that appeals to slaves, with its talk
of the meek inheriting the earth. I can assure you that
the only thing my slaves will inherit when I die is a
modest sum and perhaps their freedom if they deserve
it! Christians want to see themselves as slaves, for some
inexplicable reason. They say they are the slaves of their
Christ and they call their god 'master'. But for all their
talk of charity and alms-giving you should not imagine

that Christians treat their slaves much differently to us worshippers of the true pagan gods.

Indeed, every wealthy Christian I have ever come across owns slaves in just the same way as a normal Roman of the same status would. Their church also owns slaves just as municipal councils do. And do not imagine that Christians let their slaves run riot. They tell slaves to obey their masters. And if they do not, then they beat them just as hard. I heard of one Christian woman who actually went so far as to beat her slave girl to death. Her punishment from the church authorities was to be excommunicated for five years, seven if it could be established that she carried out the act deliberately. Christians also accept the obligation to return a runaway slave to his owner. One of their leaders, a man called Paul, sent a fleeing slave who had come to him back to his owner Philemon. I believe that Paul sought to persuade the slave's legitimate owner to treat him gently (whether or not he did I have no idea and is, in any case, an irrelevance), but the important point to realise is that Paul fulfilled his legal obligation not to harbour a fugitive.

Christians share our low opinion of slaves. Those Christians who see themselves as intellectuals are always attacking the alleged vices of the wealthy members of their sect. They say they are acting as badly as their slaves do; that they show the same typical vices of their slaves, who are often thieves and runaways, or are completely dominated by their appetites and by greed. They take it as read that slaves are bad, just as we Romans tend to do. They share our understanding of how morally inferior slaves, almost by definition, must be. Of course, they also share our view that it is possible for even the basest and grubbiest individual to act virtuously. But these acts are exceptions that prove the rule, not anything more.

Christians are, in truth, often slaves themselves. Or they come from a servile background. Even one of their supreme leaders, whom they call pope, was once nothing more than a fraudulent slave. Apparently, there was a certain slave called Callistus, who happened to be the slave of a wealthy man called Carpophorus. Carpophorus was a Christian believer but also belonged to the emperor's household, to which he owed his fortune. One day he handed over a large sum of money to Callistus, since he believed him to be a reliable person. He instructed him to set up in business as a banker in the public fish market. Before long, various Christians had deposited substantial deposits with him, since he was backed by the financial might of the emperor's associate Carpophorus. But Callistus secretly spent it all, and, having no money of his own, found himself in a dreadful fix.

But someone found out and told Carpophorus, who came to Callistus and demanded that he present his accounts for inspection. Callistus, seeing the danger he was in, was terrified and so decided to run away by escaping across the sea. He found a ship at Portus ready to set sail and went on board happy to go wherever the ship was heading. But someone spotted him and told Carpophorus what had happened. Carpophorus hurried down to the harbour and tried to board the ship. Fearing the dreadful punishments that would await him if he were recaptured, Callistus threw himself into the sea to kill himself. But everybody on the shore started shouting and the sailors jumped into their small boats and pulled him out reluctantly. He was handed back to his rightful owner and carted off to Rome.

Furious at his fraudulent incompetence, his master put him to work on the treadmill. But after a while some fellow Christians approached Carpophorus and pleaded with him to release the runaway from his punishment. A kindly man, he eventually relented and released him on condition that Callistus pay back the money he had lost. But Callistus had no money and since he was unable to escape again, as he was being kept under guard, he decided again to try to kill himself. Or rather he decided to get himself executed. So one Saturday he went to the synagogue where the Jews assemble and started causing a commotion. The Jews were upset by his behaviour and started insulting and beating him. Then they dragged him off to the urban prefect Fuscianus, complaining that this Christian had caused a public disturbance. The judge was furious but, again, someone told Carpophorus, who came to the court and informed the judge that the slave was simply a fraudster who wanted to get himself killed because he had stolen a lot of money. But the Jews assumed that this was a trick on the part of Carpophorus to have his slave released. So they appealed to the prefect in an even more hostile manner. He gave in to them, had Callistus whipped and sentenced to be sent to the mines in Sardinia.

Even here this slave's tricks did not stop. There were other Christians in the mines, who had high connections in the imperial household. Callistus managed to get in with them and they all got their freedom. But the bishop

of Rome, who had arranged the release, was so embar-
rassed when he discovered that he had unwittingly freed
a known criminal that he sent Callistus off to Antium
with a monthly allowance. And they say crime doesn't
pay! In the end, this wicked and deceitful slave became
an administrator in the Christian church and finally the
pope himself. This is the kind of person who leads the
Christians: a man of the lowest social rank, matched only
by the baseness of his morals.

I understand that the Christians want to change a few
things about how slaves are treated. They believe it is
wrong that, when slaves are sold, families can be broken
up. They say that if a Christian ever became emperor –
as if! – he would decree that when slaves are sold, then
the husband and wife, parents and children, would have
to be sold together. And he would outlaw the practice
of branding runaway slaves on the face. But you should
note that the reason for wanting to do this is not out of
sympathy with the fugitives, for they are criminals, but
so that the face, which is, in the Christian view, made in
the image of the countenance of their one god, should
not be scarred or disfigured. So Christians would prefer
that slaves be branded on the foot or leg instead. I believe
they also wish to decree that any slave forced into prostitution by her master should automatically become free.

Christians certainly do not believe that there should
be no slaves, unlike that squeamish Alan who caused me
to write this book. But they share with us the view that
it is only right that slaves who have given many years
of good service deserve to be freed. I understand that
their practice is to do this at their Easter festival, after a

slave has served them for six years. The Christian church often helps in facilitating manumission. For in the eyes of most Christians the ecclesiastical court of a bishop has the same, if not more, authority as the law courts of the Roman state.

Christians always seem to be obsessed with sex and the same is true when it comes to slaves. Some of them seem to think it is wrong for a master to share the beds of his slaves. They argue that when the head of the household behaves like the husband of the slave girls, his wife is not far removed from the status of a slave. They say that when the head of the household behaves in an immoral way then he corrupts the morals of the slaves also. They rightly state that the master's position within his household is like that of the head to the body: his own lifestyle sets a standard of behaviour for everyone. But they go on to argue that in sleeping with their slaves, masters force slave women to behave wickedly since they have no option but to obey their masters against their will. They become slaves to another's lust. It is the usual Christian nonsense. And you would be very naive if, in reality, you believed that wealthy Christian slave owners did not also behave like that. And why shouldn't they? After all, was there any whose slave girls did not enjoy their master's visits?

·· COMMENTARY ··

Early Christian writing is full of imagery drawn from slavery. The Latin word for Lord (*Dominus*) is the same as that used for 'master'. The word for 'redemption' is the same as that used in Latin for 'buying one's freedom'. The New Testament also has many sections relating to the treatment of slaves. This may reflect the fact that early Christianity was a religion of the oppressed and so had greater appeal to slaves. Alternatively, it may show that slavery was so pervasive an institution that its language got into all forms of social life, even new forms of religious expression. It may also show that many slave owners were adherents to Christianity and influenced the way it expressed itself. We must not assume that Christianity was inherently better disposed towards slaves than other earlier forms of ancient thought, such as Stoicism.

We would like to think that Christian teachings improved the conditions of slaves. But it is not clear from the evidence that Christian owners treated their slaves any better than did pagan masters. Many Christian writers seem to be as oblivious to their slaves as were pagan writers. In Luke 7:1–10 Christ heals a centurion's slave and praises the former's faith. He makes no comment on the status of the latter. And Christian authors assume that slaves will behave immorally. We therefore find numerous examples where Christian writers compare the bad behaviour of their flock to the kind of behaviour you would normally expect from a slave. But, like Stoic writers, Christian texts often emphasise that slaves were also capable of acting morally.

St Paul took great care not to fall foul of the Roman law by harbouring a fugitive. He sent back a runaway slave to his owner Philemon. Paul's concern is to ensure that Philemon acts leniently towards his slave. This does at least show that there was a Christian ideal that a master should behave decently towards his slaves. Yet this kind of ideal also existed in the sort of pagan philosophy we saw in Chapter IV. Did this have much influence on the lived reality on the ground? It's impossible to say.

Paul also told slaves that they should obey their masters. But he said, too, that their suffering was comparable with that of Christ. This emphasised how good were their prospects of future salvation. There is no hint that slaves should rebel or even resist their condition. Instead they are told 'to be submissive to their masters and to give satisfaction in every respect; they are not to talk back, not to pilfer, but to show complete and perfect fidelity' (Paul's *Letter to Titus* 2: 9–10). Some later Christian writers, such as John Chrysostom, interpreted Paul's sending back of the slave to Philemon as meaning that slavery should not be abolished.

The conversion of the emperor Constantine to Christianity in AD 312 did not make much difference to the plight of slaves. He did pass laws preventing the splitting-up of slave families at sale (*Theodosian Code* 2.25), forbidding the branding of slaves on the face, and prohibiting slaves being used as prostitutes by their masters. This last law reflects the Christian concern with the body as a site of morality. This meant that a master's sexual behaviour towards his slaves acquired a significance it had not held for a Roman audience.

It was not until the late fourth century that Gregory of Nyssa provided the first Christian text that attacks slavery as an institution (*Fourth Homily on Ecclesiastes*). Many have seen this as the first ancient text, pagan or Christian, to call for the abolition of slavery, although it is not clear that he is taking what would have been an extreme position for its time. He may simply have been trying to persuade Christian owners to treat their slaves better. Even if he is arguing for abolition, his remained a lone voice in antiquity.

The story of the crooked slave Callistus, who was later to become pope, from *c.* AD 217–222, is told by his rival Hippolytus (in *The Refutation of All Heresies* 9.12.1). This means that we should probably take the story with more than a pinch of salt. It also underlines that we should be careful about seeing one universal Christian attitude towards slavery. Christian views of slavery were as varied as those of the Romans, and changed significantly over time.

An example of a Christian sermon assuming that slaves are morally inferior can be found in Salvian *The Governance of God* 4.3. For stricter Christian attitudes towards the sexual exploitation of slaves by their masters see also Salvian 7.4. The Christian emperor Constantine's law against forcing a slave into prostitution is in the *Theodosian Code* 15.8.2. Paul sending back the runaway slave Onesimus to his owner is in his *Letter to Philemon*.

FAREWELL!

T HESE THEN ARE THE PRINCIPLES that apply to the ownership and management of slaves. If you have read and studied my words with the same care and diligence you should expect of your slaves, then you will have acquired the knowledge you need to manage an efficient and successful household. You will know how to command authority and demand respect among your underlings. You will know something of the theory of slavery. You will understand what makes a slave function well, how best to treat him, and how best to get pleasure from your assets. You will know when the time is right to set your slaves off on the path of freedom, as loyal clients to your cause. You will also appreciate the pitfalls that occupying a high-status position and a leadership role can bring. But you will be all the better able to avoid them. In short, you will know how to be the Master.

·· COMMENTARY ··

No one now argues, like Falx, that slavery is acceptable or justifiable. But before we congratulate ourselves on how far we have come, we should remember that it is a tragic fact that even though slavery is illegal in every country in the world, it still exists widely. The NGO Free the Slaves estimates that there are 27 million individuals who are forced to work under threat of violence, without pay or hope of escape. There are more slaves in the world today than there were at any point in the life of the Roman empire.

FURTHER READING

GOOD TRANSLATIONS OF THE PRIMARY texts
can mostly be found in the Loeb Classical Library or
Penguin Classics. The three sourcebooks listed below
also contain a range of textual selections relating to
ancient slavery. The original Latin and Greek texts are
most easily accessed in the Loeb Classical Library, which
has a facing translation. More thorough editions of the
original sources can be found in the Teubner series.

General works on ancient slavery

Finley, M. I., *Ancient Slavery and Modern Ideology*, revised ed.
by B. D. Shaw, Princeton, NJ: Markus Wiener Publishers,
1998.

Finley, M. I. (ed.), *Classical Slavery*, with a new introduction
by W. Scheidel, London: Cass, 1999.

Garnsey, P., *Ideas of Slavery from Aristotle to Augustine*,
Cambridge: Cambridge University Press, 1996.

Heuman, G., and Burnard, T., (eds), *The Routledge History of
Slavery*, Abingdon, Oxon: Routledge, 2011.

Sourcebooks

Lewis, N., and Reinhold, M. (eds), *Roman Civilization: A
Sourcebook*, New York: Harper Row, 1966.

Shelton, J., *As the Romans Did: A Sourcebook in Roman Social History*, Oxford: Oxford University Press, 1998.

Wiedemann, T. E. J., *Greek and Roman Slavery*, London: Croom Helm, 1981.

Works on Roman slavery

Beard, M., 'Ciceronian Correspondences: Making a Book out of Letters', In T. P. Wiseman (ed.), *Classics in Progress: Essays on Ancient Greece and Rome*, Oxford: Oxford University Press, 2002, pp. 103–44.

Bradley, K., *Slavery and Rebellion in the Roman World 140 B.C.–70 B.C.*, Bloomington, Ind.: Indiana University Press, 1989.

Bradley, K., *Slavery and Society at Rome*, Cambridge: Cambridge University Press, 1994.

Bradley, K., *Slaves and Masters in the Roman Empire: A Study in Social Control*, Oxford: Oxford University Press, 1984.

Fitzgerald, W., *Slavery and the Roman Literary Imagination*, Cambridge: Cambridge University Press, 2000.

Glancy, J. A., *Slavery in Early Christianity*, Oxford: Oxford University Press, 2002.

Harper, K., *Slavery in the Late Roman World, AD 275–425*, Cambridge: Cambridge University Press, 2011.

Harris, W. V., 'Demography, geography and the sources of Roman slaves', *Journal of Roman Studies*, 89 (1999), 62–75.

Hopkins, K., *Conquerors and Slaves*, Cambridge: Cambridge University Press, 1978.

Hopkins, K., 'Novel evidence for Roman slavery', *Past & Present*, 138 (1993), 3–27.

Joshel, S. R., *Slavery in the Roman World*, Cambridge: Cambridge University Press, 2010.

Mouritsen, H., *The Freedman in the Roman World*, Cambridge: Cambridge University Press, 2011.

Rathbone, D., 'The slave mode of production in Italy',
    Journal of Roman Studies, 73 (1983), 160–68.

Scheidel, W., 'Human Mobility in Roman Italy, II: The Slave
    Population', *Journal of Roman Studies*, 95 (2005), 64–79.

Scheidel, W., 'Quantifying the sources of slaves in the early
    Roman Empire', *Journal of Roman Studies*, 87 (1997),
    156–69.

Schiavone, A., *Spartacus*, trans. J. Carden, Cambridge, Mass.:
    Harvard University Press, 2013.

Shaw, B. (ed. and trans.), *Spartacus and the Slave Wars: A Brief
    History with Documents*, Boston, Mass.: Bedford, 2001.

Toner, J., *Popular Culture in Ancient Rome*, Cambridge: Polity,
    2009.

Wiedemann, T. E. J., *Slavery* (Greece & Rome New Surveys
    in the Classics 19), Oxford: Clarendon, 1987.

Works on Greek slavery

Cartledge, P. A., 'Like a worm i' the bud? A heterology of
    classical Greek slavery', *Greece & Rome*, 40 (1993), 163–80.

Cartledge, P. A., 'Rebels and Sambos in Classical Greece:
    A Comparative View', in P. A. Cartledge & F. D. Harvey
    (eds), *Crux: Essays Presented to G.E.M. de Ste. Croix on his
    75th Birthday*, London: Duckworth, 1985, pp. 16–46.

Finley, M. I., 'Was Greek civilisation based on slave labour?',
    in his *Economy and Society in Ancient Greece*, B. D. Shaw
    and R. P. Saller (eds), London: Chatto & Windus, 1981.

Fisher, N. R. E., *Slavery in Classical Greece*, Bristol: Bristol
    Classical Press, 1993.

Garlan, Y., *Slavery in Ancient Greece*, trans. J. Lloyd, Ithaca, NY:
    Cornell University Press, 1988.

Jameson, M., 'Agriculture and Slavery in Classical Athens',
    Classical Journal, 73 (1977–78), 122–45.

Osborne, R., 'The economics and politics of slavery in Athens', in A. Powell (ed.), *The Greek World*, Abingdon, Oxon: Routledge, 1995, pp. 27–43.

Smith, N. D., 'Aristotle's theory of natural slavery', *Phoenix*, 37 (1983), 109–23.

Wood, E. M., *Peasant-citizen and Slave: The Foundations of Athenian Democracy*, London: Verso, 1988.

INDEX